NEW DIRECTIONS IN PUNCHED METAL JEWELRY

20 CLEVER AND EASY STAMPED PROJECTS

AISHA FORMANSKI

INTERWEAVE.
interweave.com

EDITORS ERICA SMITH AND BONNIE BROOKS
TECHNICAL EDITOR CHLOE CHATENEVER
PHOTOGRAPHER JACK DEUTSCH
STYLIST RAINA KATTELSON
ASSOCIATE ART DIRECTOR JULIA BOYLES
COVER AND INTERIOR DESIGN KARLA BAKER
PRODUCTION KATHERINE JACKSON

Interweave
A division of F+W Media, Inc.
201 East Fourth Street
Loveland, CO 80537
interweave.com

Maufactured in China by RR Donnelley Shenzhen.

Library of Congress Cataloging-in-Publication Data
Formanski, Aisha.
New directions in punched metal jewelry :
20 clever and easy stamped projects /
Aisha Formanski.
    pages cm
Includes index.
ISBN 978-1-59668-723-3 (pbk.)
ISBN 978-1-59668-943-5 (PDF)
1. Jewelry making. 2. Punching (Metal-work)
I. Title.
TT212.F67 2013
745.594'2--dc23

2013009031

10 9 8 7 6 5 4 3 2 1

ACKNOWLEDGMENTS

I would like to thank my friends and family. Writing this book was possible because of your love and support. In addition, a special thanks to Lisa Niven Kelly, Bevin McNamara, Mindy Prabhu, Jesse Willenbring, and my partner, Nicholas Shuminsky.

CONTENTS

INTRODUCTION

I had moved to California's Bay Area from Minnesota in October of 2010, specifically in search of reawakening my creativity in jewelry making. After high school, I attended Minneapolis Technical College Jewelry Manufacturing program and then Revere Academy of Jewelry Arts where I was trained as a traditional metalsmith. Since then I had spent many years focused on fiber art and other jewelry-making techniques such as Precious Metal Clay, seed bead weaving, and wirework. But I felt a strong pull to get back to my metalworking roots. Living in the Santa Cruz Mountains allowed me to grow as an artist and experiment with new ideas, practices, and designs as a metalsmith again.

Inspiration ended up coming when I least expected it! While having my hair cut at a local salon in town, I was mesmerized by the huge antique Mexican copper-framed mirror in front of me. Its size and detailed texture, in dark patinated metal, was striking. I inquired about the piece and the stylist explained that it had been salvaged by the salon's owner and was very, very old. I saw it had been made using the traditional rustic style of punched-tin home decor. Established in the 1800s, this method of craftsmanship used tin sheet metal to create decorative mirrors, light fixtures, and lanterns. The chance encounter with this enormous mirror instantly inspired me to try to re-create this technique in jewelry, putting a creative spin on the established techniques of punching.

Like punched tin home decor, the character of punched jewelry is expressed through the decoration and manipulation of metal. A punch tool is used to drive an impression into a metal sheet, creating designs in patterns and words. In my studio, I searched through craft supplies looking for clues on how I could merge the techniques of punched jewelry with the aesthetic of the Mexican mirror. Armed with a glue stick, graph paper, a sheet of metal, and my steel punches, I got to work.

As I explored punching and texturing sheet metal, I found myself drawn to embroidery patterns. It was exciting to translate stitches traditionally made on fabric with thread to indentions on sheet metal made with steel stamps. By experimenting with these methods and ideas, changing the punched pattern and physical design, I could explore a wide range of styles. I started creating stamped patterns on metal that surprised me with their depth and interest. Every time I completed the stamping and removed the graph paper, a beautiful new one-of-a-kind pattern was revealed. The possibilities of creating geometric patterns with a cool, rustic feel seemed infinite.

THE TECHNIQUES OF THIS BOOK

One of the great things about this style of jewelry is that it's based on a very simple technique. After you gain familiarity with a few simple tools and materials and read Chapter 2, The Punching Technique (see page 16), you'll be ready to start experimenting with creating designs—whether you follow the templates provided at the back of the book or choose to create your own personal designs.

Chapter 3, Metalworking Techniques (see page 22), introduces other basic jewelry-making methods, so you can start creating more layered designs. The techniques include riveting, shaping, sawing, and hole punching. They're simple enough for anyone to learn, and they open up a world of possibility as you follow the project instructions in this book and later begin to design your own patterns.

Following those chapters, you'll find twenty one-of-a-kind jewelry projects—bracelets, earrings, rings, necklaces, charms, and findings—for you to create using the new skills you've learned. Patterns are provided so you can re-create the intricate overall designs used in the projects.

All of the projects in this book can be made using commercially available steel punches.

In the end, you'll have the joy and satisfaction of making and wearing beautifully made punched jewelry pieces—handcrafted by you! So let's get started.

DIFFICULTY LEVELS

■■■ BEGINNER

Any level of jewelry maker can feel comfortable with this level of project. Some of the techniques covered at this level are: shaping, punching holes, and adding a patina to your finished work.

■■■ INTERMEDIATE

Once you have a few basic techniques under your belt you're ready for the intermediate-level projects. These projects will introduce you to riveting and take you further into shaping techniques and cutting with shears.

■■■ ADVANCED

These are projects that have many different techniques in one design, including riveting and sawing.

CHAPTER 1
TOOLS &
MATERIALS

The tools I list in this chapter are all you need for a full-fledged cold-connection jewelry studio. Here's my advice to those of you who are just starting out:

- Pick and choose what you invest in by choosing a handful of techniques you would like to learn first. This way, your initial investment won't be as large, and you can add as you advance in your learning.

- Alternatively, or in addition to the above, after you learn the basics of the punching technique (see Chapter 2 and the tools listed in this chapter), you can simply choose one of the many beginner-level projects in this book and acquire the tools and skills needed for it. Slow and steady wins the race. Soon enough you'll have worked through all twenty projects, from beginner to advanced, and you'll have a full library of tools at your disposal!

THE BASIC TOOLS FOR PUNCHING

These are core tools you'll need if you're interested in achieving the effects of the punched metal pieces in this book but have less of an interest in cutting, forming, and shaping metal. You can easily create your own designs, and some variations on these designs, using precut blank metal shapes available at craft and bead stores.

STEEL STAMPS

Decorative stamps made of steel are used to create impressions in metal. For most of the patterns in this book, you'll be making textured patterns using stamps that create impressions of dashes, curves, dots, and other shapes, combining them in interesting ways.

Stamps also are available for many different styles of lettering—uppercase and lowercase, in fonts both standard and whimsical. Lettering is a great way to bring a personal touch to your work.

There are plenty of design stamps available to use for the punching technique. Expand your design options by collecting a variety of design stamps. Then change the look of a pattern by changing the design stamp in the instructions to a new design. Doing so creates a million design options and makes your punched designs truly yours.

In Chapter 2, you'll learn about the punching technique, putting your stamps to good use.

STEEL STAMPS

SETTING UP YOUR HOME STUDIO

While in school, I had become comfortable using large equipment in a traditional jewelry studio. After jewelry school, though, I no longer had access to a studio and had trouble wrapping my mind around how to translate my needs into the limited space of a small apartment. I started researching portable and affordable equipment used in cooking, ceramics, and woodworking.

In my studio at home, I have a jeweler's bench and various worktables that suit my needs. I started thinking about making a more portable jeweler's bench that would be more accessible and more affordable, and I came up with this!

I ultimately purchased a butcher-block-top kitchen cart from a big-box furniture store.

The cart is perfect because it is stable, small, and portable. Because it has wheels on two of the floor legs it is easy to roll to an area that's appropriate. If I need ventilation, I move near a window. When I do my punching and stamping I can move to an area of the house where the sound is absorbed best. The height of the cart is great for sawing. I attached my bench pin to the edge of the table and am at a comfortable height to avoid stressing my shoulder and arm muscles.

The two shelves hold my tools organized by technique or categories I see fit: metal stamps, hammers, files and sandpaper, soldering tools, sheet metal, and cutting and sawing tools. My flex shaft hangs from a stand that is attached to the back side of the cart. My most-used tools stay at arm's reach, hung from a towel bar attached to the top edge of one side of the table.

Here is a list of the design stamps used in this book.

✳	4 Petal—Cross Star	2.5mm × 2.5mm
✳	Asterisk	1.6 mm × 1.6 mm
○ ○ ○	Circle Set	2 mm, 4 mm, and 6 mm
⌣	Crescent Burst	6 mm
◗	Elongated Teardrop	5.5 mm × 2 mm
✲	Heart with Wings	5 mm × 2 mm
⅄	Medium Tripod	3 mm × 3 mm
•	Period	1 mm
♥	Plain Heart	2 mm × 2 mm
–	Short Dash	.5 mm × 2 mm
╲	Slash	.5 mm × 4 mm
)	Small Curve	Parenthesis, 1 mm × 4.5 mm
⌒	Thin Arch	6 mm
◔	Tiny Teardrop	1.5 mm × 2.5 mm
∨	"V"	6 mm

DESIGN STAMPS

ENDLESS POSSIBILITIES

Stamps also come in a huge array of images: animals, holiday motifs, flowers, and random objects (camera, sneaker, hot air balloon). If you can dream it, there's probably a stamp for it!

BRASS MALLET AND BENCH BLOCK

BENCH BLOCK

A bench block, also called simply a steel block, is a high-quality block made of steel. It's used as a solid base for work while punching your pattern, texturing, flattening metal, and riveting. For this technique, I prefer a 4" × 4" (10 × 10 cm) bench block.

BRASS MALLET

A 1-pound brass mallet is used to strike the steel stamp and drive an impression into metal. When it strikes a steel stamp, the brass mallet has sufficient density and heft to give the stamp a bounce-less blow and create a consistent impression, avoiding double and partial impressions.

POUNDING MAT

To keep the steel bench block from damaging your worktable, and also to soften the sound of striking the punches with a hammer, I use a thick dense rubber mat called a Poundo Mat.

SHAPING

Once you have the basics of the punching technique down pat, you can start to expand your repertoire with other tools and techniques. Shaping metal is one key way to add dimensional quality to your finished pieces.

DAPPING BLOCK AND PUNCH SET

This tool creates domed discs when you sandwich a metal disc between a punch and the block, then strike it with a hammer. Dapping punches are rounded, polished steel stakes that come in a variety of sizes. The accompanying block has various-sized concave circles into which the dapping punches fit. Dapping punches and blocks are available in metal and wood. I generally use metal because you can create a dapped disc quickly and consistently. The only downside is that if you inadvertently overstrike the piece, you may end up damaging the pattern that you had stamped on the metal.

NYLON-JAW PLIERS

These pliers have a nylon jaw attached to both sides of the pliers allowing for manipulation of metal without marring.

WRAP-AND-TAP PLIERS

Three different-sized barrels allow for a variety of circle and ring-shaping possibilities. The plain side of the pliers is covered with PVC tubing to protect your work from being damaged while shaping. I use large and medium size wrap-and-tap pliers in this book.

NYLON BRACELET-BENDING PLIERS

These pliers have a nylon convex upper jaw and a concave lower jaw used to shape bracelets from sheet metal or wire.

NYLON RING-BENDING PLIERS

These pliers have deep nylon convex and concave jaws that form wire or sheet metal into a circular finger-ring shape.

STEEL MANDRELS

The hardened steel ring and bracelet mandrels are for measurement and forming.

SANDBAG

I use a sandbag to support the steel ring mandrel to give resistance while I rivet and to prevent damage to the piece while working. The side effect to using this tool is dampening the sound.

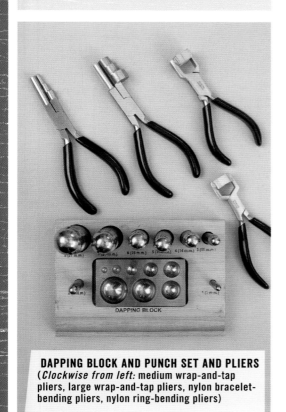

DAPPING BLOCK AND PUNCH SET AND PLIERS
(*Clockwise from left:* medium wrap-and-tap pliers, large wrap-and-tap pliers, nylon bracelet-bending pliers, nylon ring-bending pliers)

STEEL MANDRELS AND SANDBAG

CUTTING

Cutting is an essential skill for making punched metal pieces. After you create patterned sheets, you can cut them into beautiful shapes, even layering them if desired. To get the right look and feel for your cut pieces, you have many tools available.

METAL SHEARS

Whether your design needs a sharp edge or rounded corner, you'll need a handy way to create those cuts. Shears cut sheet metal just as scissors cut paper. They work well for cutting straight lines and larger shapes. Shears cut thin sheet metal up to 20-gauge. (Gauge is the thickness of the metal; the larger the gauge number, the thinner the metal.)

JEWELER'S SAW FRAME, SAW BLADES, AND CUT LUBRICANT

The jeweler's saw is a U-shaped frame with a handle; its two clamping nuts tighten to hold a saw blade. These tools are used together to saw through metal. Lubricating your blade and drill bit lets the blade or bit travel smoothly through the metal. (See Chapter 3 for more detailed instructions on using the jeweler's saw.)

BENCH PIN WITH CLAMP

This tool attaches to your worktable, supporting the piece you're sawing or drilling while allowing it to be rotated.

FLUSH CUTTERS

The blades of flush cutters are angled to cut wire flush, leaving a clean end. You can purchase single- or double-flush cutters. Single-flush cutters cut one side of the wire flush. Double-flush cutters cut both sides of the wire flush. Flush cutters will save you time when finishing the ends of your wire. Do not use your flush cutters to cut beading wire because the wire's steel core will dull your cutters.

DISC CUTTER

Disc cutters come in a wide variety of sizes and are made from hardened steel. A disc cutter cuts shapes from sheet metal, up to 18-gauge in soft metals. (See Chapter 3 for more detailed instructions on using the disc cutter.)

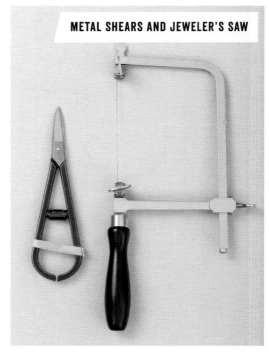

METAL SHEARS AND JEWELER'S SAW

BENCH PIN WITH CLAMP

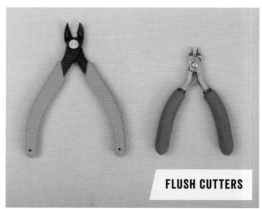

FLUSH CUTTERS

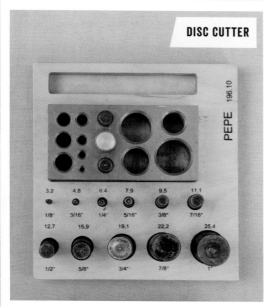

DISC CUTTER

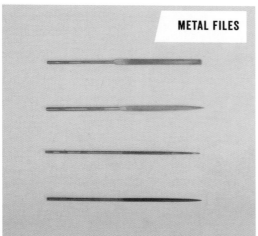

METAL FILES

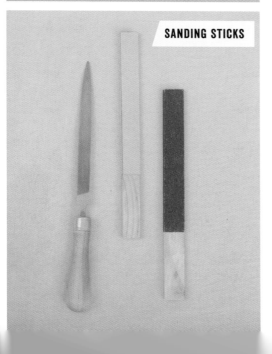

SANDING STICKS

FILING AND SANDING

It's important to file and sand your pieces well. Your jewelry should not have sharp corners that could injure the wearer. For your pieces to be cleanly finished, you want to file and sand away all burrs and sharp edges.

METAL FILES

Metal files come in many different shapes, sizes, and grades of coarseness. Needle files are for small places, to clean up rough or sharp edges created by cutting or drilling the metal. Large files will cover a larger area and remove material more quickly. The most common shapes of metal files are round, half round, flat, square, and triangular. Match the shape of the area you're working on with the shape of the file.

Most jewelry files have the coarse cut facing one direction. This means that you should file in one direction only, against the grain of the file. File on the push stroke, not the pull stroke: start at the tip of the file and move the piece toward the handle. Support your piece against your bench pin, rubber block, or other surface to create a bit of resistance.

SANDPAPER, SANDING PADS, AND SANDING STICKS

These items can be used to smooth out slightly rough edges and corners. A few good options include traditional wet/dry sandpaper; emery boards, which are wooden sticks with fine-grit sandpaper attached; and sanding pads. All come in a variety of grits, and for these projects, you'll be working with 300 grit and finer. Flat sandpaper can be used to help in creating a smooth and flat surface by laying the paper flat on the table and sanding the piece in a figure-eight shape. This motion creates a consistent removal of material.

MAKING HOLES

When you make jewelry, you're always adding holes to connect components, add findings, weave through, or create a cold connection. You can create holes in metal many ways, but using simple hole-punch pliers, a manual drill, and a screw-down hole punch are the easiest.

SCREW-DOWN HOLE PUNCH

This tool gives you two hole-size options in one tool, 1.6 mm and 2.3 mm. The screw-down hole punch is very easy to use, and the two hole sizes it creates are commonly needed. This punch can be limiting, though, because its insertion depth is shallow.

HOLE-PUNCH PLIERS

These pliers are easy to use and come in a variety of sizes. They have one small drawback: hole-punch pliers can leave a mark on the surface of the metal around the hole. This happens because the little stump on which the punch pin is mounted strikes the metal when you punch the hole. You can avoid this marking by placing a thick piece of cardstock over the stump the pin is mounted on. Some hole-punch pliers come with a guard to prevent this from happening.

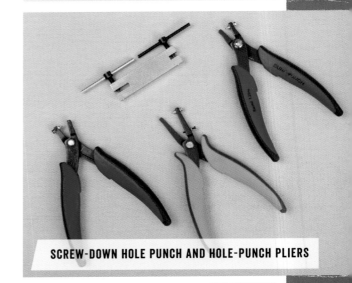

SCREW-DOWN HOLE PUNCH AND HOLE-PUNCH PLIERS

HAMMERING

Hammers have so many uses in jewelry making. These hammers will assist you when you create cold connections as well as when you texture and manipulate metal.

RIVETING HAMMER

This hammer has a chiseled end and a slightly domed side and is used to flare and flatten rivets.

DEAD-BLOW MALLET

Dead-blow mallets allow flattening and light shaping of metal without distorting the metal's surface. I use a rubber mallet for the projects in this book, but they are also available in rawhide, plastic, and urethane.

CHASING HAMMER

This hammer has one slightly convex face for forging or work-hardening handmade findings. The other end is round for riveting and for creating a traditional "hills and valleys" hammered texture on metal.

HAMMERS (*From left to right: riveting hammer, dead-blow mallet, chasing hammer*)

PLIERS

Jewelry pliers are a must-have when making jewelry. They're small and have smooth jaws and comfortable handles—quite different from what you find at a hardware store. Specialty jewelry pliers are designed to assist in making a particular curvature, or to assist in making a well-finished piece.

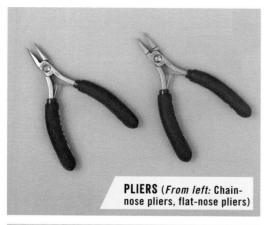

PLIERS (*From left:* Chain-nose pliers, flat-nose pliers)

PLIERS SET

A set of jewelry pliers includes chain-nose, flat-nose, and round-nose pliers.

- **Chain-nose pliers** have a tapered (and sometimes bent) tip to optimize dexterity while gripping and bending small items, such as chain links or wire loops.
- **Flat-nose pliers** provide a firm grip on flat objects and create sharp bends and angles in wire or metal.
- **Round-nose pliers** have round mandrels, ideal for creating wire loops or rounded bends in metal.

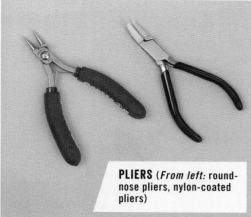

PLIERS (*From left:* round-nose pliers, nylon-coated pliers)

NYLON-COATED PLIERS

These pliers are useful when you manipulate metal and need to protect the piece from being marred. They come in various nose shapes.

POLISHING

In this book, I teach a very basic polishing technique that doesn't require motor tools or an advanced polishing tutorial. You'll simply use #0000 steel wool to create a slightly scratched rough surface or Pro Polish Pads to polish the metal to a fairly high shine.

STEEL WOOL

This fine-grit abrasive material is used to remove patina or to create finely scratched surfaces on metal. I often use it on pieces when I want to create a more organic look.

PRO POLISH PADS

These special foam pads have a bonded micro-abrasive. They're great for removing tarnish and oxidation as well as for polishing. They should only be used dry, so make sure your jewelry is completely dry before using a pad.

STEEL WOOL AND PRO POLISH PADS

MEASURING TOOLS

CIRCLE DIVIDER

This tool is used to divide a circle evenly. Place your piece in the middle of the circle and use a permanent marker to mark the necessary divisions.

RULERS AND MEASURING TAPE

A ruler, millimeter gauge, bracelet gauge, and measuring tape will be essential to measuring your jewelry in a variety of increments.

THE LITTLE THINGS THAT BRING IT ALL TOGETHER

GLUE STICK

A water-based glue adheres the punched pattern templates to sheet metal or metal blanks.

SCISSORS

Regular craft scissors cut the patterns down to the needed size.

PLASTIC TEMPLATES

These plastic shape templates are convenient when cutting out shapes from metal sheet. Retail sources for plastic templates are listed on the Resources page in the back of the book.

TOOTHBRUSH

An old toothbrush will help remove very small pieces of the paper pattern that may remain in the impressions of the stamping.

PERMANENT MARKER

A fine-point permanent marker is used often while fabricating your finished piece. Use the marker to place marks on the surface of the metal. This will help when punching holes, cutting sheet metal, and planning out your punching. Permanent marker can be easily removed from the surface of metal with a Pro Polish Pad or fine steel wool.

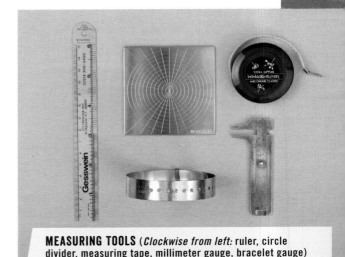

MEASURING TOOLS (*Clockwise from left:* ruler, circle divider, measuring tape, millimeter gauge, bracelet gauge)

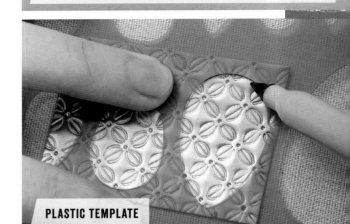

PLASTIC TEMPLATE

OPTIONAL TOOLS

The tools listed below are luxury tools. They will assist you in production if and when you become completely addicted to making jewelry.

Drill: A non-motorized hand drill can be used with a C-clamp with plastic or rubber jaws to drill holes in sheet metal. Use the C-clamp to clamp your working piece against a scrap piece of wood before drilling.

Tube-Cutting Jig: This tool supports and holds the tubing while you saw the length you desire. A groove in the holder lets you center the tubing to saw a precise length.

SHEET METAL

MATERIALS

SHEET METAL

You can use a variety of metals for punched metal jewelry. Throughout this book, I use copper, brass, bronze, and both silver-filled and sterling silver. I also use several thicknesses of sheet metal throughout the book, including 20-, 22-, and 24-gauge. Gauge describes the thickness of the metal: the larger the number, the thinner or smaller the gauge.

WIRE

Wire comes in a wide variety of gauges and materials. I use copper, silver-filled, and sterling silver for the projects in this book. Expand your designs by mixing metals.

RIVETS

Nail-head rivets and eyelets come in a variety of different metals and sizes. I use 1/20" (1.3 mm) diameter nail-head rivets and 1/16" (1.58 mm) diameter eyelets in the projects included in this book.

FINDINGS

To finish the designs, you'll need a small variety of ear wires, clasps, jump rings, bead cones, and chain. Jump ring sizes are described in two ways—inner diameter (ID) and outer diameter (OD). Be aware of the sizing when you purchase jump rings.

RIVETS AND FINDINGS

ABOUT THE METALS

Brass, an alloy of copper and zinc, has a yellow color.

Bronze, an alloy of copper and tin, has a dark golden-brown color.

Copper is very soft and malleable.

Silver-filled is created when a solid layer of sterling silver is heat-and-pressure bonded to a core of copper or brass.

Sterling silver contains 92.5% pure silver and 7.5% of a mixed alloy, mostly copper.

CHAPTER 2
THE PUNCHING TECHNIQUE

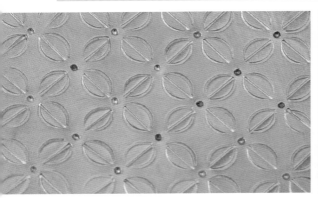

Even if you're a novice jewelry maker, punching metal using steel stamps is a skill that can be picked up easily and will take you far. Punching is a relatively simple process that can be expanded upon as you go. Using just this one technique, you have the means to create an infinite variety of patterns.

To be specific, "punching" means creating impressions in metal using steel stamps. To create the pieces in this book, you'll create repetitive geometric patterns following a template on a patterned sheet. I've included a collection of patterns for your use in the back of the book. They can be used to duplicate or build onto the design to add your own elements. I also go over using the grid pattern to create your own designs and experimenting with freeform or free-hand punching.

After learning just a few basic skills and techniques, you will embark on an adventure in creating beautiful jewelry.

GETTING THE SWING OF IT

Practice before you begin with your project, even if you're experienced in stamping. Every time I come back to my stamping station, I practice a little before getting started.

Experiment with the way you carry out your hammer blow. Some people get the perfect impression with one or two strikes and others use a jackhammer style. It all depends on your arm strength and your comfort level.

You can use a Poundo Mat below the bench block to deaden the sound of striking the steel stamp.

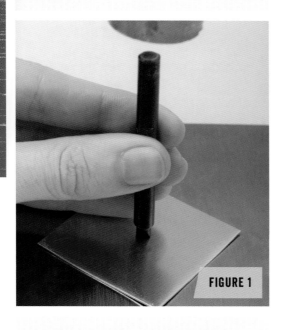

FIGURE 1

USING THE DEAD-BLOW MALLET

The dead-blow mallet is used only sometimes when the metal becomes warped from a lot of punching and needs to be flattened out, or metal needs to be formed without being damaged at the same time.

HOW TO PUNCH

Letter and design stamps are made from hardened steel. By striking them with a brass mallet into soft metal, you create an impression. A few important tools are needed for successful stamping. You'll need a sturdy table, a bench block, a brass mallet that is 1 lb or heavier, and a dead-blow mallet.

To stamp metal successfully, it's important to practice. Every time I sit down to stamp letters or designs, I practice first on inexpensive copper sheet. This gets me familiar with the specific stamps I'll be using for my design and warms up my hammering arm.

TOOLS
Bench block
Steel stamps
Brass mallet
Dead-blow mallet

1 Place the bench block on a sturdy table and sheet metal on top of the bench block. Hold the steel stamp in your nondominant hand and position the stamp on the sheet metal. You don't want to hold the stamp completely at the top because doing so will make the stamp tip. Make sure that you have a good grasp on the stamp at the bottom of the stamp, one that lets you support the stamp against the sheet metal.

2 With the brass mallet in your dominant hand, strike the top of the steel stamp, creating an impression in the metal (**Figure 1**). The depth of the impression will depend on the strength of the strike.

3   If you strike the stamp too lightly, or you don't make full contact with the stamp when you strike it, you may get only a partial impression. If this happens, you can slide the stamp into the partial impression and strike the stamp on the side that didn't impress. If you strike the stamp too hard, you'll create an unnecessarily deep impression that could almost break through the back side of the sheet metal. This will create punched sheet metal that is distorted and structurally unsound. If this happens, just take a deep breath and try again! **Figure 2** shows a partial impression and a too-deep impression.

4   Once you have completed your punching, your metal may be warped from the manipulation of the metal. Lightly hammer the punched piece positioned on the bench block with a dead-blow mallet. This will flatten the metal out once again. You can also use the dead-blow mallet in the middle of punching if you're punching a large piece and feel that it would make continuing your punching easier.

FIGURE 2

ADJUSTING YOUR APPROACH

If you don't create the impression you were hoping for, try making small adjustments to solve the problem; use a heavier or lighter hammer, try tilting the stamp toward the area where you're not getting an impression, then strike the stamp. If you're not satisfied, double-check that you have the proper tools to be successful.

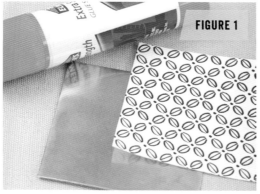

FIGURE 1

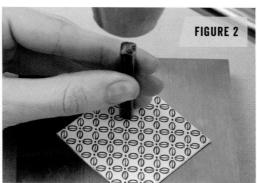

FIGURE 2

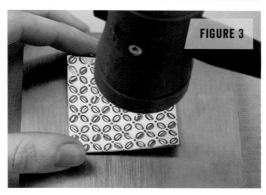

FIGURE 3

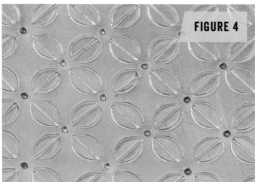

FIGURE 4

HOW TO USE A PATTERN

TOOLS
Pattern
Scissors
Water-based glue stick
Stamps
Brass mallet
Dead-blow mallet
Warm water
Toothbrush

1 Photocopy a pattern from the back of the book or use your own paper pattern. The patterns are designed to match the punches listed in Chapter 1, so make sure you photocopy the patterns at 100%.

2 Trim the pattern down to the size you'll need for your project.

3 Adhere the pattern piece to the sheet metal with a water-based glue stick (**Figure 1**). Burnish the paper down with your fingers to ensure the paper makes full contact with the sheet metal. Allow time for the glue to dry before starting to punch—about 20 minutes.

4 Punch out the pattern using the brass mallet and the steel stamps required to create the pattern (**Figure 2**). If the pattern calls for you to create an asterisk in the center of an allover design, create those impressions first. Then go back and add each additional element to the design. This will create consistent strikes and therefore a consistent punched sheet.

5 The more you punch, the more warped your sheet metal will become. As you work, lightly tap your sheet metal all over with a dead-blow mallet to flatten it back out (**Figure 3**).

6 When you have completed your punching, flatten the sheet metal one more time using the dead-blow mallet. Run warm water over the pattern and rub away your pattern as it dissolves under the running water. There will be small pieces of the paper pattern left in the deep impressions of the punching. Use a toothbrush and scrub the punched piece under running water. When you are done, your piece will be bright, shiny, and clean (**Figure 4**).

THINGS TO REMEMBER

- While punching, if you find that you've lost your place, you can flip the piece over and see where your impressions are and where you need to continue punching.

- When you punch, work from left to right, or from the top down. When you look at the pattern, decide that you're going to start with the simplest punch inside the pattern—such as the dot. Work either toward the left side or the top of the pattern and focus on only punching that particular stamp. Then go back and add to it.

- As you stamp, feel free to interpret the pattern as you see fit. The more detail you add, the more interesting your final punched sheet will be. For this reason, don't panic if you "mess up" and punch something incorrectly. In many cases, you can simply incorporate the unintended punch into the pattern.

MAKING YOUR OWN PATTERNS

In the back of the book, you'll find a blank graph paper pattern (see page 124). This is intended for you to photocopy, adhere to sheet metal, and play with as you start to design your own patterns.

When you design your own patterns, I encourage you to start with a main impression in the center and work your way out. For example, I like to start by placing an impression in a diamond formation. From there, I add smaller lines and dots. I have found that the more impressions you add, the better the design becomes. Make a photocopy of the punched sheet and save an original. You can then duplicate and build upon the design.

You have endless choices when it comes to patterns. Find a pattern on a skirt in your closet, on your favorite mug, or at the playground and pull inspiration from there.

In this book, I'll cover using printed geometric patterns, embroidery patterns, and freehand designs, as well as designing your own patterns on graph paper.

EMBROIDERY PATTERNS

Embroidery patterns and other printed patterns may also be used. But if you reproduce patterns, it's important that you pay close attention to the designer's copyright statement, ask permission to use them, or use copyright-free images.

In the Hello Owl Wall Piece (at left), I used (with permission) an embroidery pattern from Sublime Stitching, which offers a huge variety of patterns. I purchased the pattern online, printed it out, and resized the image on a copy machine. I then cut out the elements of the pattern I wanted to use and glued them onto the sheet metal. Embroidery patterns work beautifully for this punching technique because you can interpret each stitch as a steel stamp design and expand on the original design.

STUDIO SAFETY

Sometimes, the small inconveniences of safety discourage us from following through on proper handling of materials and precautions. I have listed below the basic safety precautions I use in my own studio. Always follow the manufacturer's safety instructions for any tool you use; see page 32 for safety precautions with the use of patina.

STRETCH!

A healthy body equals great jewelry and a happy jewelry maker! When working at your worktable or jeweler's bench for extended periods of time, take breaks. Stand up and stretch your back, legs, and arm muscles. Make sure you're sitting at a comfortable height in a chair that supports your back and allows your feet to be planted firmly on the ground.

EARPLUGS

You will be using a heavy hammer, and the strike of the stamp against the steel bench block can be very loud. I recommend wearing earplugs to protect your hearing.

PRACTICE

It's also a good idea to practice striking the steel stamp with the hammer. This will get you comfortable wielding a hammer and will prevent accidently hitting a finger.

SAFETY GLASSES

When cutting sheet metal and wire, small parts of metal do unexpectedly fly up. You must wear safety glasses.

CHAPTER 3

METALWORKING
TECHNIQUES

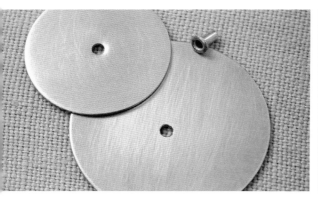

Once you have punched your patterns, you'll be
ready to move into creating one-of-a-kind jewelry.
The metalworking techniques I've included here
are the foundation of traditional jewelry making.
Once learned, these simple techniques will serve
you well.

In jewelry making, you can create the same result many ways.
I describe the techniques in this chapter as I execute them; this is
how I've practiced them in my studio for years. However, I encourage you to experiment and find other ways that suit you and your
designs. Go for it!

CUTTING METAL

Cutting sheet metal can be a simple task when done with the right tool. You can cut, pierce, or saw shapes in sheet metal many ways. You can use metal shears, a jeweler's saw, and even a large guillotine-style cutter to cut down large quantities of sheet metal. I use the metal shears and a jeweler's saw every time I work at my bench. These two tools allow you to create custom shapes. Metal shears are used as scissors are used to cut paper (see Chapter 1), but using a jeweler's saw requires additional setup and practice.

USING THE JEWELER'S SAW

For more detailed designs, you may want to use the jeweler's saw. This is a "must-have" tool that is worth mastering. Though you'll most likely find it awkward while you're learning, you'll undoubtedly find a comfortable rhythm quickly. Sawing makes cutting shapes and finishing so much easier than alternative methods of cutting.

Begin by attaching your bench pin to your worktable. This tool lets you saw freely while giving you the freedom to rotate the piece you're working on in any direction necessary. Ideally, the bench pin will be at the same height as the bottom of your shoulder while you're seated, putting minimum stress on your arms and shoulders while sawing for extended periods of time.

The jeweler's saw is adjustable to accommodate a range of saw-blade lengths. The saw has three wing nuts: one loosens the frame to shorten or lengthen it to accommodate a range of saw-blade lengths, and the other two open and close the two jaws at the top and bottom to clamp the end of your saw blades into the frame.

Saw blades are small and come in a variety of sizes. Insert your saw blade with the teeth facing outward and down toward the handle of the saw frame. The teeth on these blades are very small. To check that you have inserted the blade in the correct direction, you can lightly run your finger over the teeth from the top of the saw to the handle; it will feel smooth. You'll create the cut on the downward pull stroke, so this placement is essential.

To insert the saw blade and cut:

1 Position your jeweler's saw between your worktable and you, loosen the top wing nut, and insert the blade with the teeth facing outward and down toward the handle (**Figure 1**).

2 Tighten the wing nut.

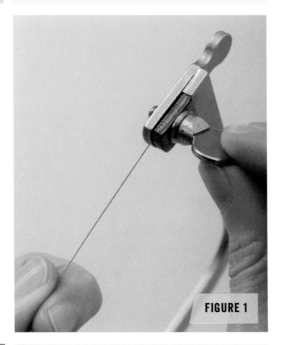

FIGURE 1

3 You need to create some stability and pressure in order to insert the bottom part of the blade. I do this by pressing the top of the saw frame against the side of the worktable and wedging the handle against my shoulder or breastbone. Alternatively, you can place the top of the saw frame against the top of your worktable and press down on the saw handle. Whatever method you choose, you can now insert the bottom part of the blade into the second wing nut. The tension you've created will keep your blade taut. You can pluck the blade to check the tension. You want to hear a high-pitch pling, not a low and clunky plunk.

4 Apply a liberal amount of cut lubricant to the blade's teeth.

5 When you first start sawing, you'll most likely hold the jeweler's saw handle with what I call a "death grip." Instead, try to keep a very loose hold on the handle, allowing the handle to be cradled in the nook between your thumb and pointer finger. Let the blade do the work while sawing. If you hold the handle too firmly and press against your piece, trying to force the blade forward, all you'll get are broken blades and a sore shoulder.

6 Use a fine-point permanent marker to mark your piece of sheet metal where you want to saw and position the sheet on your bench pin. Support it against the bench pin with your nondominant hand. Place the saw blade against the sheet metal at a 45-degree angle to the bench pin and lightly pull down (**Figure 2**).

7 Once you have the cut started, straighten your frame up and saw forward in a gentle up-and-down motion. To turn a corner, saw in place while slowly rotating the piece with your nondominant hand.

SAW-BLADE CHART

Each thickness or gauge of metal will need a different-size saw blade to cut it efficiently. Think of it like biking; if you have the right momentum, gear, and conditions, biking can be a breeze. But if you're riding uphill in the wrong gear in the rain, you may never want to ride your bike again. It's important to have the right-size saw blades, lubricant, and bench pin. You can use the chart I've included at right, or you can follow the "two teeth" rule, which is that you need to have two teeth of blade equal to the thickness of the metal you're using.

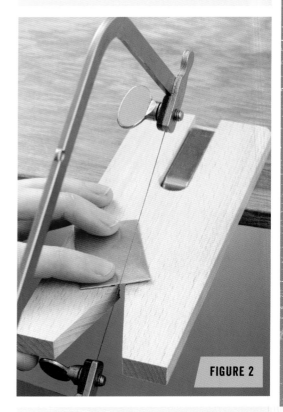

FIGURE 2

METAL GAUGE	SAW BLADE SIZE
26-gauge	8/0
24-gauge	6/0
22-gauge	4/0
20-gauge	2/0
18-gauge	1
16-gauge	2

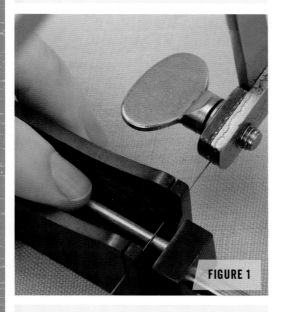

FIGURE 1

SAWING TUBING

To cut tubing, use a tube-cutting jig and a jeweler's saw. Measure and mark the tubing to the desired length using a fine-point permanent marker.

Insert the tubing into the tube-cutting jig, adjust the stopper to accommodate the total length of the tubing, and center the mark in the slot.

1   Hold the jig with your nondominant hand against your worktable and use the jeweler's saw to saw the tubing apart (**Figure 1**).

2   Once the tubing is cut, use sandpaper to make smooth the ends of the tubing, sanding in a figure-eight motion. I use this technique in the Josephine Crescent Necklace project (see page 74) to make my own tube rivets.

ADDITIONAL HOLE-PUNCHING TECHNIQUES

There are several easy ways to make holes in metal.

SCREW-DOWN HOLE PUNCH

This single-hole punch can make holes of two sizes: it makes a 1.6 mm hole, which fits 14-gauge round wire, and a 2.3 mm hole, which fits a 12-gauge round wire. This tool can cut through soft metals up to 14-gauge. Because it has a shallow insert, you won't be able to create a hole farther than ⅝" (1.5 cm) from the edge of your metal using the 1.6 mm side and ⅜" (1 cm) from the edge of your metal using the 2.3 mm side.

To use the screw-down hole punch:

1   Using a fine-point permanent marker, mark your metal where you would like to punch your hole. Place the metal in the tool, positioning the punching pin above your mark (**Figure 1**).

2   Slowly screw the pin down through the metal until you feel the turning loosen. This is the indication that you have successfully punched through the metal.

3   Back the pin out of the metal, being careful that your piece doesn't whip around and get scratched by the top of the tool.

DRILL

■ When you drill, you always want to lubricate the bit. Doing so will allow the bit to travel more smoothly through the metal.

■ A manual hand drill can be used just like a household drill. I suggest you first clamp your working piece to a piece of wood that is then attached to a table with a C-clamp. This will keep your working piece from getting stuck on the drill bit and allow you to drill your hole successfully.

FIGURE 1

SMOOTH PUNCHING

Replace worn punch pins in the screw-down hole punch and hole-punch pliers often to avoid creating inconsistently sized holes. If the hole you create has small sharp pieces of metal surrounding it, hold the drill bit in your hands and slowly twist the bit into the hole. This will quickly remove any sharp bits of metal.

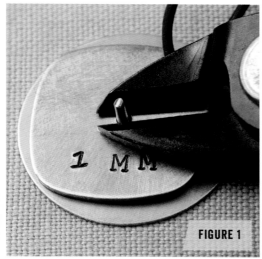

FIGURE 1

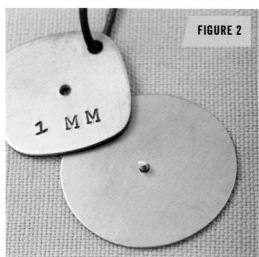

FIGURE 2

RIVETING

Riveting is what's called a "cold connection," a join that traditionally uses wire, a nail, or a tube to connect multiple components. Riveting involves flaring the end of a piece of round metal material until the metal "mushrooms" out, filling the hole that runs through the components and connecting the pieces together.

RIVETING TILES

When you're riveting, it's important that the length of the rivet is the same every time. For this purpose, I make little rivet-sizing tiles using 24- and 18-gauge blanks. Twenty-four-gauge measures almost .5 mm thick and 18-gauge measures almost 1 mm thick. In this case, I use 1" (2.5 cm) rounded square blanks. I drill a hole in each tile and use the tiles to assist in cutting the same size rivet every time. I stamp the thickness and gauge into the blank with a steel letter and number set.

When you're ready to trim down a rivet wire, you'll first have a length of rivet sticking up out of your project (represented here by a blank round disc).

1 Thread the tile onto the rivet wire, place your flush cutter against the tile, and trim (**Figure 1**).

2 Remove the tile, and, depending on which tile you used, you'll have either .5 mm or 1 mm of rivet remaining (**Figure 2**).

WIRE RIVETING

This riveting technique uses round wire to create a cold connection. By threading the wire through your components, you can simply connect them with very few tools. Wire rivets are great to use when you want the finished rivet head to have a low profile, or when you want to control the size of the hole you create to rivet through. Just match the gauge wire to the hole size.

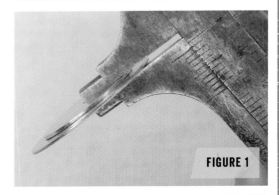

FIGURE 1

1   Create a hole only slightly larger than the gauge wire you would like to use. One of the most important factors when riveting is that your wire fits tightly in its hole.

2   Use a sliding gauge to measure the thickness of your components (**Figure 1**) and add 1–2 mm to that measurement. This is how long your wire rivet needs to be. Measure and mark your wire (**Figure 2**) and cut with a flush cutter, making sure both edges are flush cut flat.

OR

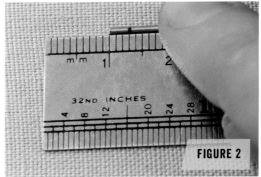

FIGURE 2

3   Using the riveting tile as described on page 27, flush cut one end of the wire, then slide your components onto the wire. Use the riveting tile and flush cut the second end of the wire. If there is any remaining unevenness, lightly file the ends.

4   Place your working piece on a bench block. Using the chisel side of the riveting hammer, strike the top of the wire, and move the strikes across the top, rotating the top to create a consistent "mushrooming" or flaring (**Figure 3**).

FIGURE 3

5   Once the rivet begins to flare slightly, flip the piece over and begin to flare the second side. You want to slowly rivet each side, flipping to the other side of the rivet every few strikes. Doing so will ensure similar-sized rivet heads on both sides of your work.

6   Once the rivet is mostly flared on both sides, flip the hammer to the smooth side. Strike the rivet until it is flush against the working piece (**Figure 4**).

FLIP IT

It's important to flip your work often as you rivet two pieces together. If you don't, the rivet will wedge and not come through on the flip side.

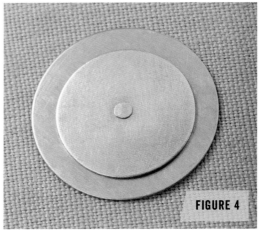

FIGURE 4

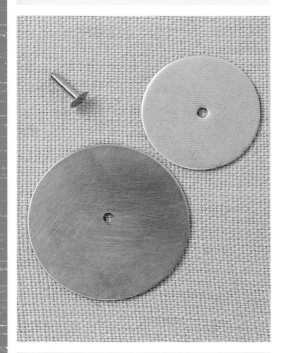

NAIL-HEAD RIVETS

Ready-made nail-head rivets are easy to use. They're ideal when you need to place a rivet but will be unable to rivet both ends due to tight spaces, such as those on a ring. On a ring, you would be able to strike the rivet wire on the exterior of the ring, but not in the interior.

1   Create a hole only slightly larger than the gauge of the nail-head rivet you would like to use. The nail-head rivets I use in this book fit perfectly when you use the 1.5 mm hole-punch pliers. Using the riveting tile as described, flush cut the rivet down to .5–1mm in length. Thread your nail-head rivet through the hole.

2   Place the rivet head on a bench block and flare the rivet wire with the chisel end of the riveting hammer. Strike the top of the rivet, moving the strikes across the top of the wire, and rotating the rivet to create a consistent "mushrooming" or flaring until the rivet is mostly flared. (See **Figure 3** on the previous page.)

3   Once the rivet is mostly flared, flip the hammer to the smooth side, striking the rivet until it's flush against the working piece.

TUBE RIVETING

This technique makes a cold connection using a tube. Using tubing leaves an open hole in the center of the rivet to thread a jump ring through or add another design element to your piece.

1   Create a hole slightly larger than the tubing you'll be using. Because tubing is normally a lot larger than standard gauge wire, you may need to create a large hole for it. For the specific tubing I used in the Josephine Crescent Necklace, you can use the large end of the screw-down hole punch. Or you could create a hole with whatever tool you have handy, then open the hole up to the size you need using a round file.

2   Measure the thickness of your components and add 3–4 mm to that measurement to get the necessary length of your tube rivets.

3   You'll cut your own length from a length of tubing. With tubing, you'll need to use a tube-cutting jig and a jeweler's saw to cut it, then sand the ends smooth (refer to Sawing Tubing on page 25)

4   Place the tube in the hole you've created and slightly flare one edge using a flaring tool (you can also use a period stamp, shown) against a bench block (**Figure 1**). Flip the piece over and do the same on the back side.

5   Using the flat side of the riveting hammer, tap the flare down against the piece until it's smooth to the touch (**Figure 2**).

EYELET RIVETING

An eyelet rivet is a tube rivet with one end already flared. Eyelet rivets are great for adding an industrial-look cold connection quickly. (The centers of pre-flared eyelet rivets are smaller than the centers would be if you made your own eyelet rivets from tube rivets.)

1   Create a hole slightly larger than the eyelet rivet, using the small end of a screw-down hole punch.

2   Thread the eyelet through the hole and with a metal file, file the eyelet length down to 2 mm.

3   Using a flaring tool, slightly flare the non-flared end of the eyelet against the bench block.

4   Using the flat side of a riveting hammer, tap the flare against the piece until it's smooth to the touch.

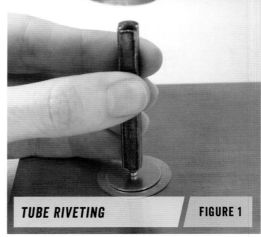

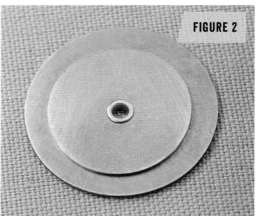

TUBE RIVETING — **FIGURE 1**

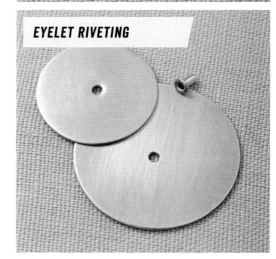

FIGURE 2

EYELET RIVETING

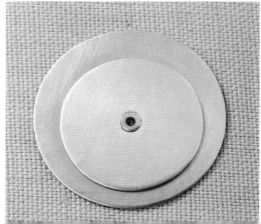

DAPPING · FIGURE 1

FIGURE 2

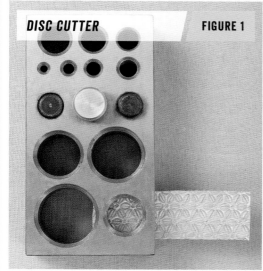

DISC CUTTER · FIGURE 1

FIGURE 2

DAPPING

Dapping is used to create domed pieces of metal. There are wood and metal dapping sets, which come with a dapping block and punches. Both wood and steel sets are good for specific needs. I use a wood dapping and punch set with a dead-blow mallet when I shape thinner gauges, such as 24-gauge; I use a metal dapping and punch set with a heavy hammer when I need to shape thicker metals.

To use a dapping set to shape metal:

1   Place your piece either faceup or facedown in the largest well (**Figure 1**), depending on the design you're building. If you want the design on the domed/convex side, place the piece facedown in the dapping block well. To keep the pattern on the concave side (**Figure 2**), place the piece face outward in the dapping block well.

2   Lightly strike the punch with the hammer many times, rotating the punch so it comes in contact with all areas of the piece, being careful not to over-strike. If you over-strike, you could possibly distort the punched pattern.

3   To create a deeper curvature, continue to the next size well and punch, always making sure that the punch and well match in size.

DISC CUTTER

These steel disc cutters let you cut a circle from the sheet metal you've punched your pattern into.

To use the disc cutter:

1   Insert the sheet metal into the side slot of the disc cutter. The metal should be fully visible through the opening of the hole you wish to punch (**Figure 1**).

2   To help the punch cut through the sheet metal more easily, add a moderate amount of lubricant to your punch.

3   Use a heavy metal hammer or brass mallet to strike the punch. You'll most likely need to strike the punch several times until the punch pops through the metal sheet (**Figure 2**).

CHAPTER 4

ADDING
PATINA & SEALANT

You've learned how to make impressions in your metal, but it's the contrast of dark grooves on brighter surfaces that will give your pieces depth and interest. Adding antiquing, patina, or oxidation and then polishing the top surface of the metal leaves the color in the impressions and makes the punched pattern pop from the surface. Many processes can change the color of your metal.

Some patinating solutions or agents may be harmful if used without proper safety measures. I suggest getting the Materials Safety Data Sheet (MSDS) for any patina from your jewelry tool supplier or from the manufacturer directly. You can always research the ingredients online. Also, wear rubber gloves, safety glasses, and an apron and work in a well-ventilated area when you work with chemicals that change the color of metal.

DARKENING SOLUTIONS (*Clockwise from left:* liver of sulfur, silver blackener, permanent marker)

DARKENING SOLUTIONS

LIVER OF SULFUR

What it is: This traditional material for oxidizing metal is used in large and small production studios. Liver of sulfur comes in liquid, gel, and rock form, contains potassium sulfide, and is very stinky— it smells of rotten eggs!

What it works with: Liver of sulfur works best with sterling silver, silver-filled, and copper.

How you use it:

1   Follow the mixing ratio on the instructions that accompany the liver of sulfur. In a small plastic container, mix the liver of sulfur with hot water. You want the water to be as hot as your tap water at its hottest. (I don't suggest you boil the water. Doing so causes the liver of sulfur to bond very thickly to the surface of the metal, and it will be extremely hard to remove.)

2   Submerge your pieces in the liver of sulfur bath. You can drop them straight in and fish them out with a plastic spoon, or you can use a steel wire basket to dunk them in and out of the bath.

3   Once your pieces have reached the color you like, rinse them in a solution of one part baking soda to ten parts water. Make sure your pieces are dry before proceeding further. For most pieces, you can remove excess liver of sulfur with a Pro Polish Pad. In the case of copper, though, you'll need to use a coarser option, so you can use #0000 steel wool. During this part of the process, you can choose how you want the surface of the piece to look by leaving or removing the coloring.

4   After your liver of sulfur bath has cooled to room temperature, cover and store it in a safe place. Add enough hot water next time you want to use it to warm the bath.

NEUTRALIZING LIVER OF SULFUR FOR DISPOSAL

You can neutralize liver of sulfur by adding baking soda. Begin by adding a small amount of baking soda to your liver of sulfur. This will cause the solution to bubble. Continue to add more baking soda until the bubbling stops. Then dispose of it down the toilet. If you have a septic system contact your service company to ask if this method is appropriate. The safest method is to place your open container of liver of sulfur in a safe place to evaporate.

BLACKENING AGENTS

What it is: A blackening solution (common commercial products include JAX, Black Max, and Silver Black) that contains hydrochloric acid and tellurium, which makes it very harmful; handle this solution with extreme caution. Please read the MSDS on any blackening agent before you use it. Of the many silver-blackening solutions on the market, Griffith Silver Black is my favorite.

This agent works best on sterling silver and silver-filled, but it can be diluted with water to allow it to adhere to copper and brass.

To use on sterling silver and silver-filled:

1   Unscrew the cap and dip a cotton swab into the liquid, saturating the swab. Lightly brush your piece with the cotton swab. Your metal will turn black immediately.

2   Once you have finished swabbing, let the piece dry.

3   Dip the used cotton swab and piece in a baking soda and water bath of one part baking soda to ten parts water to neutralize the Silver Black, then throw away the cotton swab.

To use on copper and brass:

1   Pour a small amount of Silver Black into the container's cap.

2   Place the cotton swab in water and then dip it into the cap. Lightly brush your piece with the cotton swab. The metal will turn black immediately. If you have problem areas where the solution isn't adhering, add more water to the cotton swab and re-dip into the cap.

3   Neutralize the solution in the cap, the cotton swab, and the piece in a baking soda and water bath of one part baking soda to ten parts water. Do not pour remaining solution back into the bottle.

PERMANENT MARKER

Permanent marker is a quick way to add black to the impressions from the punching. Press firmly so the tip of the marker gets deep down into the impressions. Then polish off any excess marker with a Pro Polish Pad or #0000 steel wool. The results of this method aren't permanent and may come off after a piece is submerged in water often or for a long period of time.

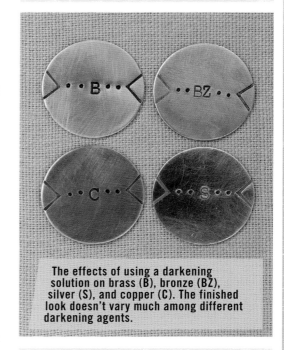

The effects of using a darkening solution on brass (B), bronze (BZ), silver (S), and copper (C). The finished look doesn't vary much among different darkening agents.

SEALANTS

Sealants can be used to protect your patina and to protect the wearer's skin from turning green from copper, brass, or nickel jewelry pieces. Few patinas are permanent, and you'll find that sealing the finish prolongs the life of the patina. Also, we're using alternative metals such as copper and brass, and these metals tend to oxidize quickly. Adding a sealant to the finished piece guarantees that it will retain its original patina.

RENAISSANCE WAX

Originally formulated in the British Museum laboratories in the 1950s to assist in restoration work, Renaissance Wax creates a thin layer that will protect from wear or damage to your patina. Rub on a light coating with a soft cloth to seal your patina.

JEWELRY SHIELD

When I make jewelry with metals that may turn the wearer's skin green, I coat the side of the piece that will come into contact with skin with Jewelry Shield. It's also great for people with metal allergies; it puts a protective coating between the metal and the wearer. This product dries clear and shiny.

CHAPTER 5

PROJECTS

MATERIALS

3¼" × ¾" (8.5 × 2 cm) piece of 24-gauge copper sheet

5–8" × 1" (12.5–20.5 × 2.5 cm) piece of 22-gauge copper sheet (exact size will depend on the size of your wrist)

1" (2.5 cm) of 14-gauge copper wire

TOOLS

Glue stick

Brass mallet

Bench block

Dead-blow mallet (plastic, rubber, or urethane)

Measuring tape

Fine-point permanent marker

Ruler

Metal shears

Metal file, medium to fine coarseness #2–#5

Fine-grit sandpaper

Screw-down hole punch

Flush cutters

Riveting hammer

Nylon bracelet-bending pliers

Liver of sulfur

#0000 steel wool

PUNCHES

Asterisk

Period

TECHNIQUES

Punching

Cutting

Hole punching

Wire riveting

Shaping

Patinating

COMO CAROUSEL CUFF

This cuff bracelet was the first piece of jewelry I made with punched sheet metal. It was my inspiration to take the technique further, and it eventually became the sample that would open the door to writing my own book. This simple design highlights the beauty of punched metal jewelry in an understated way. You'll create two pieces that will be layered and then riveted together, then shaped into a cuff bracelet. I hope this cuff bracelet inspires you as much as it inspired me.

BEGINNER   PUNCH PATTERN 8

PUNCH THE PATTERN

1 Per the instructions in Chapter 2, adhere a copy of the pattern from the back of the book to the 24-gauge copper metal sheet. Punch the pattern over the whole piece of copper sheet and clean the metal with warm water to remove the used pattern.

MEASURE YOUR WRIST

2 Measure your wrist using a soft measuring tape. Take that measurement and subtract 1" (2.5 cm). This will be the length of the main cuff piece.

CUT OUT YOUR CUFF PIECES

3 Cut the first piece from the 22-gauge plain sheet metal. Take your measurement from Step 2—that will be the length of the cuff. The width will be 1" (2.5 cm). Transfer the measurements onto the surface of the metal using the fine-point permanent marker and ruler. Cut this cuff blank from the sheet with your shears.

4 The second cuff piece is the punched pattern piece. This should measure ¾" × 3¼" (2 × 8.5 cm). Measure and mark the dimensions and cut as in the previous step.

FILE THE EDGES

5 To smooth sharp metal edges, start by filing them with a metal file. If you need to file away a lot of excess material, choose a coarser file; if you just need to smooth a rough edge, choose a finer file. If you want to make your edges even smoother after you've filed them, sand them down with fine-grit sandpaper.

MAKE HOLES FOR RIVETS IN THE PATTERN PIECE

6 Using the smaller side of the screw-down hole punch, create four 1.6 mm holes, one in each corner of the punched pattern piece 3–4 mm from the edges (**Figure 1**). Be careful not to make the holes too close to the edge of the metal. That would create a weak area that runs the risk of over-bending or snapping when you later go to shape the cuff.

MARK FOR RIVETING

7 Center the punched patterned piece on top of the cuff blank. Using the fine-point permanent marker, mark the placement of one of the holes in the patterned piece onto the cuff blank (**Figure 2**).

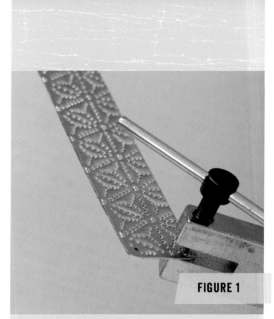

FIGURE 1

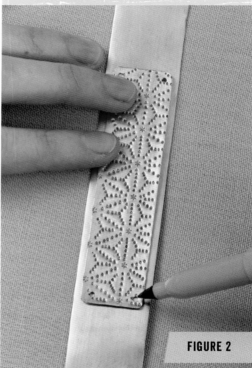

FIGURE 2

TAP IT OUT

If the cut pieces become warped from the cutting process, lightly tap them flat using a dead-blow mallet and bench block.

FIGURE 3

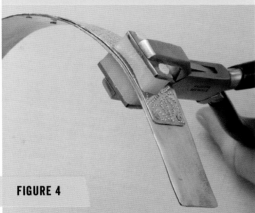

FIGURE 4

MAKE EVEN-SIZED RIVETS

No matter what length wire you choose for your rivets (.5–1.5 mm), it's important that the lengths be consistent. Create wire rivet-sizing tiles (see Chapter 3) to ensure the same length every time. In this project, you can stack two riveting tiles, 18- and 24-gauge, to get an even 1.5 mm length.

MAKE HOLES FOR RIVETING IN THE CUFF BLANK

8 Remove the punched patterned piece and use the screw-down hole punch to create a 1.6 mm hole through each mark. Place the two pieces back together faceup on the bench block.

RIVET THE TWO BRACELET PIECES TOGETHER

9 Using the flush cutters, cut a flush end on the 14-gauge wire. Place this end of the wire down through the aligned holes in the bracelet. Cut the wire, leaving 2 mm of wire above the surface of the sheet metal (**Figure 3**). This wire will become your rivet.

10 Wire-rivet the pieces together per the instructions in Chapter 3.

11 Continue to "tap and flip" the cuff until the rivet is flat against the cuff on the front and back. The longer the wire rivet, the longer it will take to flatten. For the remaining three rivets, position the punched pattern, pass the screw-down hole punch through the hole in the punched piece, and punch through the plain sheet metal. Repeat Steps 9 through 11.

SHAPE THE BRACELET

12 Using the nylon bracelet-bending pliers, curve your cuff into the shape you want for your bracelet, starting in the center and moving down both sides of the cuff (**Figure 4**). Your cuff can be oval or round—it's up to you!

ADD PATINA TO THE BRACELET

13 Use liver of sulfur to antique your cuff, then rub it with the steel wool to remove extra patina from the surface of the cuff. Voilà! You have a beautiful Como Carousel Cuff!

WEAVER STITCHED EARRINGS

I have always been drawn to crafts that use needle and thread: making the stitches always creates a soothing rhythm that I enjoy. In this vein, I've incorporated a simple wrapped wire into this earring design. The wrapping brings a textile feel into the design that makes the punched pattern pop.

■■ ■■ **BEGINNER**   **PUNCH PATTERN 1**

PUNCH THE PATTERN

1 Per the instructions in Chapter 2, adhere a copy of the pattern from the back of the book to the 24-gauge brass metal sheet. Punch the pattern over the whole piece of brass and clean the metal with warm water to remove the used pattern.

TRACE AND CUT YOUR EARRING SHAPES

2 Trace the shape of the plastic teardrop template twice with the fine-point permanent marker onto your sheet metal (**Figure 1**). Cut out your two earring pieces using metal shears. To smooth sharp metal edges, start by filing them with a metal file. If you need to file away a lot of excess material, choose a coarser file; if you just need to smooth a rough edge, choose a finer file. If want to make your edges even smoother after you've filed them, sand them down with fine-grit sandpaper.

MARK THE HOLE PLACEMENT FOR THE WEAVE

3 Use the fine-point permanent marker to mark a dot at the top and bottom of each teardrop, about ¹⁄₃₂" (1 mm) away from the edge. Following the photo as a guide and working your way up from the bottom, mark seven parallel dots spaced evenly along the edges on either side of each teardrop (**Figure 2**). You're going to have to eyeball the spacing, but a ruler or circle divider can be helpful. You can also create the quadrants first, then subdivide.

MAKE THE WEAVE HOLES

4 Punch the holes for the weave using the hole-punch pliers.

DARKEN THE IMPRESSIONS

5 Use a permanent marker to darken the punched impressions. Remove excess ink from the surface of the metal with the steel wool.

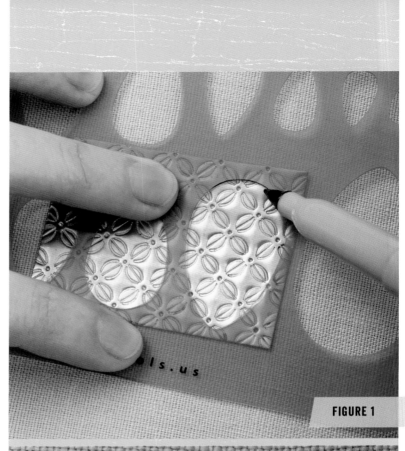

FIGURE 1

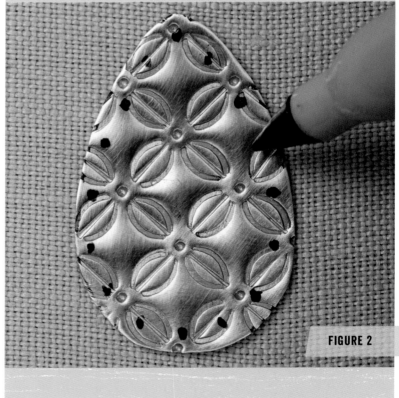

FIGURE 2

FIGURE 3

CHOOSE YOUR OWN ADVENTURE

The teardrop template chosen for this project is 1¼"
(3.2 cm) long by ¾" (2 cm) wide. However, several
templates are commercially available in different sizes.
Feel free to experiment, but keep in mind that if you make
something large, you'll need to increase the length of the
wire used for weaving.

WEAVE THE WIRE AROUND THE EARRINGS

6   Use the flush cutters to cut the wire in
half. Use one half of the wire to thread
through the first hole beside the topmost
hole in one of the stamped teardrops,
passing through the hole from back to
front, leaving a 1" (2.5 cm) tail. Wrap the
wire from front to back and pass through
the same hole again, creating two wire
loops through the hole (**Figure 3**). Bring
the working end of the wire to the back of
the earring and pass it through the next
hole from back to front. Pass through the
same hole again to create a second loop.
Work in this fashion to weave the wire
through the next thirteen holes (leaving
the topmost hole empty). Trim the wire,
leaving a 1" (2.5 cm) tail. Twist the two
tails together tightly on the back side.
Trim the wire ends and tuck the twisted
coils so they lie flat against the back of
the earring. Repeat the entire step on the
other stamped teardrop.

ASSEMBLE

7   Attach ear wires by opening and closing
their loops as you would jump rings (see
Techniques).

AUBURN DAPPED EARRINGS

These beautiful dapped earrings are a great way to show off a punched pattern. You can use circle blanks purchased from a jewelry supply company or punch out your own blanks using a disc cutter. The discs shown here are ⅞" (2.2 cm) across, but you can choose a size that suits you. No matter how you slice it, you'll have fun making these quick and easy earrings.

BEGINNER   **PUNCH PATTERN 8**

PUNCH THE PATTERN

1 Per the instructions in Chapter 2, adhere a copy of the pattern from the back of the book to the circle blanks. Punch the pattern over the whole surface of each circle, and clean the metal with warm water to remove the used pattern.

FILE SHARP EDGES

2 Because you were punching over the edge of the circle blank, you will have created a few sharp edges and distorted areas on the edges. To smooth sharp metal edges, start by filing them with a metal file. If you need to file away a lot of excess material, choose a coarser file; if you just need to smooth a rough edge, choose a finer file. If you want to make your edges even smoother after you have filed them, sand them down with fine-grit sandpaper.

SHAPE THE DISCS

3 Dap the punched discs facedown using the dapping punch and block set, per the instructions in Chapter 3 (**Figure 1**). Start in the shallowest well into which a whole disc can completely fit and tap the disc with the corresponding dapping punch and a heavy hammer until it matches the curvature of the well. Move to the next well size down and repeat until you have the curvature you like.

FIGURE 1

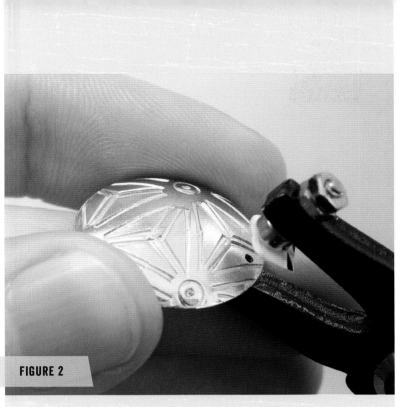

FIGURE 2

MAKE THE HOLES FOR THE EAR WIRES

4   Use the fine-point permanent marker to mark where you would like each hole to be, about ¹⁄₁₆" (2 mm) from the edge of each stamped circle. Punch the holes with the 1.25 mm hole-punch pliers (**Figure 2**). Remember that adding a chunk of cardboard to the tip of the pliers will prevent marring the metal.

DARKEN THE IMPRESSIONS

5   Use the fine-point permanent marker to darken the punched impressions. Remove excess patina from the surface of the metal with the steel wool. *Note:* I allowed the bronze to oxidize over a few days before sealing it with a sealant.

6   Attach ear wires by opening and closing their loops as you would jump rings (see Techniques).

MATERIALS

2½" × 1½" (6.5 × 3.8 cm) piece of 24-gauge copper sheet

2" (5 cm) of 18-gauge copper wire

1' (30.5 cm) of 22-gauge scrap wire (used to bind the pendant together during the riveting process and then be discarded)

3 copper 2mm crimp tubes

3 copper 18-gauge 5mm ID jump rings

16" (40.5 cm) of antique copper 2 mm ball chain

TOOLS

Glue stick

Brass mallet

Bench block

Metal shears

Fine-point permanent marker

Disc cutter

Dead-blow mallet (plastic, rubber, or urethane)

Metal file, medium to fine coarseness #2–#5

Fine-grit sandpaper

1.25 mm hole-punch pliers

Masking tape

Flush cutters

Riveting hammer

Liver of sulfur

#0000 steel wool

Chain-nose pliers

Flat-nose pliers

PUNCHES

Period

Circle: 2 mm

TECHNIQUES

Punching

Cutting

Riveting

Patinating

SYLVIA SHRINE NECKLACE

This pendant has spacers between the top and bottom pieces to make it three-dimensional; the tiered shape gives it the look of a pagoda or shrine. You can customize this piece by changing its shape or making the top and bottom pieces contrasting metals.

◼◼◼◻ **ADVANCED**   **PUNCH PATTERN 7**   **TEMPLATE SYLVIA SHRINE**

PUNCH THE PATTERN

1   Per the instructions in Chapter 2, adhere a copy of the pattern from the back of the book to the 24-gauge copper metal sheet. Punch the pattern over the whole piece of copper and clean the metal with warm water to remove the used pattern.

CUT OUT SHRINE SHAPES

2   Adhere two copies of the template from the back of the book to the punched sheet. Cut out the two pieces with metal shears and then clean the metal again to remove the pattern. To smooth sharp metal edges, start by filing them with a metal file. If you need to file away a lot of excess material, choose a coarser file. If you just need to smooth a rough edge, choose a finer file. If you want to make your edges even smoother after you've filed them, sand them down with fine-grit sandpaper.

FIGURE 1

PUNCH OUT THE CENTER CIRCLE PIECE

3   Use the fine-point permanent marker to trace a circle around the 19 mm disc cutter onto the center of one shrine piece (**Figure 1**). Place the shrine piece into the disc cutter and center the piece under the correct hole, using the traced circle as a guide (**Figure 2**). Punch the center out using the brass mallet. If you don't have a disc cutter, pierce and then cut out the center section using a jeweler's saw. To do so, use the hole-punch pliers to create a hole in the center of the punched piece, trace a circle around it using a template, thread the saw blade through the hole, secure it into the frame of the saw, and saw out the center section.

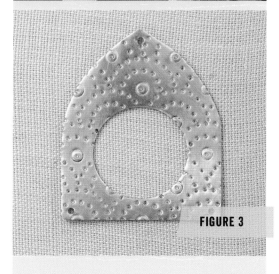

FIGURE 2

WIRE-RIVET THE METAL PIECES TOGETHER WITH CRIMP TUBES AS DIVIDERS

When you rivet multiple pieces together using many rivets, it's important to take one rivet at a time. You'll thread wires through the loosely assembled piece to hold it together while you work. Also, keep in mind that you'll be using 2mm crimp tubes as the spacers between the two layers. Be gentle when you rivet so you don't accidently collapse a tube. You'll be riveting 18-gauge wire and using a 1.25 mm hole punch to create the holes. Ideally, you want a snug fit when it comes to riveting. In this situation, there will be a little wiggle room. Once you begin riveting, pay attention that you're flaring the metal evenly to avoid the metal from working itself down crooked, or the wire falls over.

4   Use the fine-point permanent marker to mark the three spots where the rivets will be in the top metal piece, one in each point of the shrine shape, 1/16–1/8" (2–3 mm) from the edge. Use the hole-punch pliers to make the three holes (**Figure 3**).

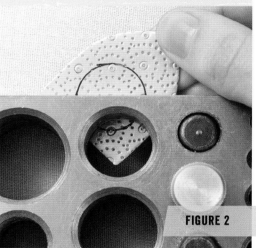

FIGURE 3

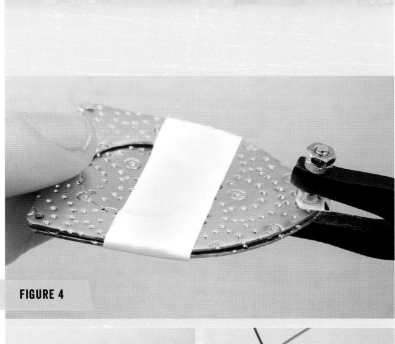

FIGURE 4

5 Tape the two pieces together. Thread the tip of the hole-punch pliers through one of the holes in the top piece (**Figure 4**) and punch holes through the bottom piece. This way, you know your holes are aligned.

SET UP FOR RIVETING

In this step, you'll create a temporary framework for keeping the two pieces spaced equally apart as you rivet them together.

6 Thread 4" (10 cm) of the 22-gauge scrap wire from back to front through a hole in the back piece, then through a crimp tube, and finally through the coordinating hole in the top piece (**Figure 5**).

7 Repeat in each set of holes, twisting the wire ends to hold each corner in place. The whole piece is now bound together (**Figure 6**).

RIVET THE TWO PIECES TOGETHER

8 Replace the holding wire in one corner with the end of the 18-gauge copper wire to wire-rivet that corner per the instructions in Chapter 3. Repeat twice to rivet the remaining corners, one at a time.

ADD PATINA

9 Use liver of sulfur to antique your pendant and then rub with steel wool to remove the patina from the top surface.

ATTACH JUMP RINGS AND CHAIN

10 Use one jump ring to attach the other two jump rings around the crimp-tube spacer on the top of the pendant (for more instruction on how to use jump rings, see page 120). Thread the chain through the second two jump rings and you're done!

FIGURE 5

FIGURE 6

MATERIALS

2 pieces of 2" × 1½" (5 × 3.8 cm) 24-gauge copper sheet

1–2" (2.5–5 cm) of 14-gauge copper wire

2 copper 18-gauge 4mm ID jump rings (large)

2 copper 18-gauge 3mm ID jump rings (small)

14" (35.5 cm) of small oval link antique copper chain

1 antique copper 6 × 10 mm lobster clasp

TOOLS

Glue stick

Brass mallet

Bench block

Metal shears

Jeweler's saw, saw blades 4/0 or 6/0 and cut lubricant

Bench pin and clamp

Dead-blow mallet (plastic, rubber, or urethane)

Metal file, medium to fine coarseness #2–#5

Fine-grit sandpaper

Fine-point permanent marker

Screw-down hole punch

Ruler

Flush cutters

Riveting hammer

Liver of sulfur

Pro Polish Pad

#0000 steel wool

PUNCHES

Period

Typewriter Uppercase 2 mm letter set

Heart with Wings

Small dash

TECHNIQUES

Punching

Sawing

Hole punching

Riveting

Letter stamping

Patinating

BELLE
PENDANT

This riveted double-sided necklace can be worn two ways. Depending on your mood, you can either show your stamped message to the world or show off your punched pattern and keep your message to yourself. Change the shape of the pendant to create your own one-of-a-kind necklace. This pendant is a great project if you want to practice sawing.

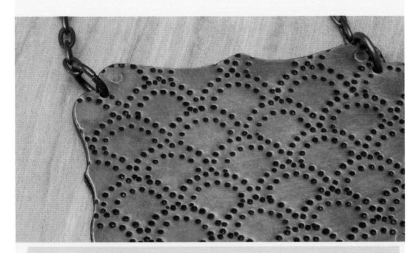

INTERMEDIATE PUNCH PATTERN 7 TEMPLATE BELLE PENDANT

PUNCH THE PATTERN

1 Per the instructions in Chapter 2, adhere a copy of the pattern from the back of the book to one of the 24-gauge copper metal sheet pieces. Punch the pattern over the whole piece of copper and clean the metal with warm water to remove the pattern.

CUT OUT THE BELLE PIECES

2 Select the template provided on page 125 or choose your own shape from a plastic template. Adhere two copies of the template to both the punched and plain metal sheets and trace them with a permanent marker. Using the jeweler's saw, cut out the two pendant pieces. If the pieces become warped from the punching process, lightly tap them flat using the dead-blow mallet and bench block.

FILE AND SAND EDGES

3 To smooth sharp metal edges, start by filing them with a metal file. If you need to file away a lot of excess material, choose a coarser file; if you just need to smooth a rough edge, choose a finer file. If you want to make your edges even smoother after you have filed them, sand them down with fine-grit sandpaper.

MAKE HOLES FOR RIVETS

4 Create a mark with the fine-point permanent marker in each corner of the punched metal piece $1/16$–$1/8$" (2–3 mm) from the edge. Using the smaller side of the screw-down hole punch, create a 1.6 mm hole through each mark and set aside.

STAMP LETTERS

5 Plan the layout of your words with the fine-point permanent marker and ruler (**Figure 1**). Using the steel letter set, bench block, and brass mallet, stamp your quote or saying (**Figure 2**). Polish the metal with a Pro Polish pad before you start stamping. Use the reflection of the letter in the metal to eyeball where you are placing the letter so it is stamped exactly where you'd like it. Remove permanent marker lines with fine steel wool.

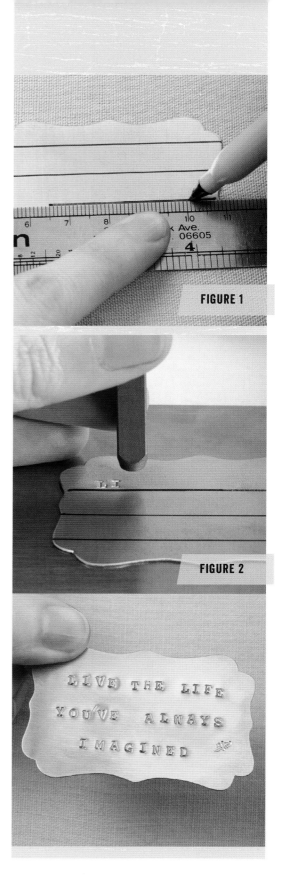

FIGURE 1

FIGURE 2

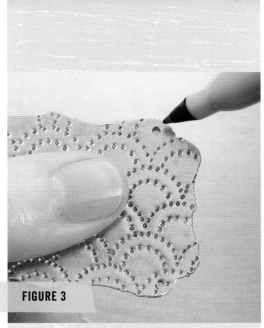

FIGURE 3

FIGURE 4

CREATE HOLES ON THE SECOND COPPER PIECE

6   Place the patterned piece on top of the letter-stamped piece, patterns facing out. With the fine-point permanent marker, mark one of the rivet holes onto the letter-stamped piece (**Figure 3**). Set aside the patterned piece and make a hole through the mark using the small end of the screw-down hole punch.

RIVET THE TWO PIECES TOGETHER

7   Place the two pieces, patterns facing out, on the bench block, with holes aligned. Cut a flush end on the 14-gauge wire using the flush cutters. Place this end of the wire through the holes in one corner. Cut the wire, leaving 2 mm of wire above the surface of the sheet metal (**Figure 4**). It is important that whatever length these wire rivets are, the length is consistent. Wire-rivet the corner wire rivet. Repeat this process three more times, passing the screw-down hole punch through the prepunched hole down into the second piece and punching a hole. Working one rivet at a time, your piece will be aligned properly.

MAKE THE HOLES FOR THE LARGE JUMP RINGS

8   Once the two pieces are riveted together, use the fine-point permanent marker to place a mark in both top corners of the pendant below the wire rivets, 1/16–1/8" (2–3 mm) from the edge of each corner. Using the small end of the screw-down hole punch, create the holes for the jump rings that will attach the pendant to the chain.

ADD PATINA

9   Use liver of sulfur (or another antiquing solution) to antique your pendant and then rub it with steel wool to remove the patina from the top surface of the pendant. If you would like to add a little shine, follow up by buffing with a Pro Polish Pad.

FINAL TOUCHES

10   When you riveted the two pieces together, they may not have been completely aligned. If you have overlapping areas, clean up any sharp parts with a file and sandpaper.

11   Cut the chain into two 7" (18 cm) pieces. Use one large jump ring to attach one side of the pendant to the last link on one piece of chain; repeat using the other large jump ring and the other piece of chain. Use one small jump ring to attach the clasp to the free end of one of the chain pieces and attach the final small jump ring to the free end of the other piece of chain.

MATERIALS

1 piece of 22-gauge brass sheet (I used a piece that was 9½" × ¾" [24 × 2 cm], but depending on your wrist size and taste, you may want to make the bangle wider or longer. Measure your wrist as described in Step 1 before you cut your sheet metal.)

1 brass eyelet, ¹⁄₁₆" (2 mm) in diameter, 3 mm long

TOOLS

Measuring tape

Ruler

Fine-point permanent marker

Metal shears

Metal file, medium to fine coarseness #2–#5

Fine-grit sandpaper

Glue stick

Brass mallet

Bench block

Nylon bracelet-bending pliers

1.8 mm hole-punch pliers

Bracelet mandrel

Riveting hammer

Sandbag

Dead-blow mallet (plastic, rubber, or urethane)

PUNCHES

4 Petal—Cross Star

Period

TECHNIQUES

Punching

Hole punching

Shaping

Riveting

BLACKWATER RIVETED BANGLE

Bangles can be worn alone or in groups—that's what makes them so versatile and adaptable to your personal style. Riveting the connection together adds an industrial look. For this design, I didn't darken the impressions. I left the punched pattern subtle, which I think creates some needed softness.

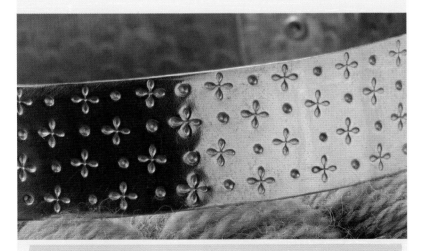

■■ ■ **BEGINNER** PUNCH PATTERN **GRAPH PAPER**

MEASURE FOR THE SIZE OF THE BRACELET

1 Measure the circumference of the widest part of your hand. Wrap the measuring tape around your hand at the base of your thumb, adjusting the tension so you can slide it on and off your hand with ease (**Figure 1**). If you pull the measuring tape too tight around your hand, the bangle will end up too small to pull over your thumb. Take a note of this measurement and add 1" (2.5 cm) for the overlap and a comfortable fit.

CUT THE BANGLE BLANK

2 Decide how wide you would like your bangle to be (the sample is ¾" [2 cm] wide). Use the ruler and fine-point permanent marker to draw your desired dimensions onto the brass sheet, using the length measurement you recorded in Step 1. Cut out the bracelet blank with the metal shears. To smooth sharp metal edges, start by filing them with a metal file. If you need to file away a lot of excess material, choose a coarser file; if you just need to smooth a rough edge, choose a finer file. If want to make your edges even smoother after you have filed them, sand them down with fine-grit sandpaper.

PUNCH THE PATTERN

3 Per the instructions in Chapter 3, adhere a copy of the grid graph-paper pattern from the back of the book to the bracelet blank. You will need to copy and then cut the graph paper into strips in order cover the total surface of the metal sheet. Strike a punch at each of the grid intersections over the entire piece of brass, alternating between the Cross Star and Period punches. Clean the metal with warm water to remove the used pattern.

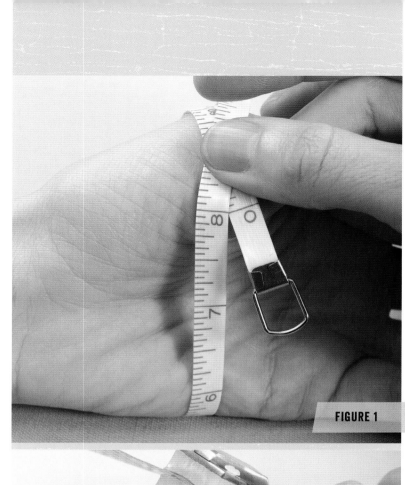

FIGURE 1

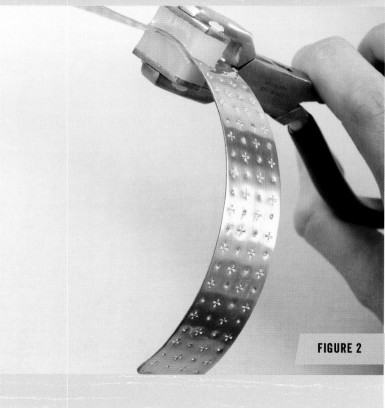

FIGURE 2

FIGURE 3

KEEP IT TOGETHER

After you thread the rivet through the holes, you can place a piece of tape over it on the inside of the bangle so it stays in place as you finish your rivet.

FIGURE 4

SHAPE THE BANGLE

4   Shape the stamped sheet using the nylon bracelet-bending pliers. Start at one end and lightly tap the pliers all the way across to the other end (**Figure 2**). The pliers won't shape the metal into a complete circle but will bend it enough to let you pinch the ends together without distorting its shape.

MAKE THE HOLES FOR RIVETING

5   Make a mark on the top side of the bangle where the eyelet will go. This should be ¼" (6 mm) from the end of the metal piece and centered widthwise. If you're making a bangle wider than ¾" (2 cm), you'll want to add a second eyelet for stability. Punch a hole through the mark using the hole-punch pliers. Overlap your bangle's ends by squeezing them together with your hand until they overlap ½" (1.3 cm), with the punched end on top and then punch a hole (through the top hole) in the bottom layer (**Figure 3**).

RIVETING THE BANGLE TOGETHER

6   Align the holes you just created and thread the eyelet through them from inside the bangle. Slide the bangle onto the bracelet mandrel and brace it on the sandbag. File the eyelet down to roughly ⅟₃₂" (1 mm) with the metal file (**Figure 4**). Rivet the eyelet rivet down per the instructions in Chapter 3.

FINISH SHAPING THE BANGLE

7   Continue shaping the bangle around the bracelet mandrel by lightly striking it with the dead-blow mallet or pressing it into shape with your hands.

MATERIALS

3" × 2½" (7.5 × 6.5 cm) piece of 24-gauge silver-filled sheet (to create twelve ⅝" [1.5 cm] discs)

4½" × ¾" (11.5 × 2 cm) piece of 24-gauge brass sheet (to create six ⅝" [1.5 cm] discs)

29 brass 18-gauge 3mm ID jump rings

2 sterling silver 15mm hook clasps

TOOLS

Glue stick

Brass mallet

Bench block

Dead-blow mallet (plastic, rubber, or urethane)

Disc cutter with ⅝" (1.5 cm) punch

Metal file, medium to fine coarseness #2–#5

Fine-grit sandpaper

Fine-point permanent marker

Circle divider

1.25 mm hole-punch pliers

Silver Black or liver of sulfur

Pro Polish Pad

Flat-nose pliers

Chain-nose pliers

PUNCHES

Asterisk

Period

Slash

Small Curve—Parenthesis

TECHNIQUES

Punching

Hole punching

Patinating

PORTAGE BRACELET

This bracelet is a great project for beginners. Punch premade blanks or make your own discs using a disc cutter, then chart your layout and link the pieces together. This linked bracelet has a lot of movement and makes for a very comfortable piece.

BEGINNER   PUNCH PATTERNS 5 & 8

PUNCH THE PATTERN

For this design, you can cut discs from punched sheet using a disc cutter (see Chapter 3 for instructions on how to use a disc cutter) or you can punch the pattern onto premade blanks.

1   Per the instructions in Chapter 2, adhere a copy of Pattern 5 to the silver-filled 24-gauge sheet. Punch the pattern over the whole sheet and clean the metal with warm water to remove the used pattern. Repeat using Pattern 8 and the sheet of 24-gauge brass sheet.

CUT OUT YOUR DISCS

2   Use the ⅝" (1.5 cm) disc-cutter punch to trace twelve circles onto the punched silver-filled sheet and six circles onto the punched brass sheet, then punch the discs. To smooth sharp metal edges, start by filing them with a metal file. If you need to file away a lot of excess material, choose a coarser file; if you just need to smooth a rough edge, choose a finer file. If you want to make your edges even smoother after you have filed them, sand them down with fine-grit sandpaper.

MARK AND MAKE HOLES IN THE DISCS

3   On the back side of the discs, mark the hole placement for the jump rings using a circle divider (**Figure 1**). Place the disc in the center of the divider, then place a small mark with the fine-point permanent marker at three of the four lines marking the quarters of the disc. When you've made three marks on each of the discs, punch a hole through each one about ⅟₃₂" (2 mm) away from the edge using the hole-punch pliers.

FIGURE 1

PATINA AND POLISH THE DISCS

4 Using Silver Black or liver of sulfur for the silver-filled metal and permanent marker for the brass, apply a dark patina over all the discs. Buff the discs with a Pro Polish Pad until the excess patina is removed from the top surface and it's shiny.

LAY OUT YOUR DESIGN

5 Establish your design by laying out your punched discs in two rows. You can use the same design shown in the sample (one pair of silver discs, one pair of brass discs, two pairs of silver discs, one pair of brass discs, two pairs of silver discs, one pair of brass discs, and one pair of silver discs) or create your own.

CONNECT THE DISCS AND CLASPS WITH THE JUMP RINGS

6 Use twenty-five jump rings to attach each pair of discs to each other and then to the next pair of discs. Use one jump ring to attach each of the hook clasps to the discs on one end of the bracelet. Attach the final two jump rings to the free holes in the discs at the other end of the bracelet.

MATERIALS

8" × 1" (20.5 × 2.5 cm) piece of 24-gauge copper sheet

18 copper 18-gauge 2.7 × 4.4mm ID oval jump rings

5 copper 18-gauge 4mm ID round jump rings

TOOLS

Glue stick

Brass mallet

Bench block

Metal shears

1.5 mm hole-punch pliers

Jeweler's saw, saw blades 4/0 or 6/0, and cut lubricant

Bench pin and clamp

Dead-blow mallet (plastic, rubber, or urethane)

Bench block

Fine-point permanent marker

Metal file, medium to fine coarseness #2–#5

Fine-grit sandpaper

Nylon ring-bending pliers

Liver of sulfur

#0000 steel wool

Flat-nose pliers

Chain-nose pliers

PUNCHES

Asterisk

Small Curve—Parenthesis

Slash

Short Dash

TECHNIQUES

Punching

Cutting

Sawing

Shaping

Patinating

CALHOUN TILES BRACELET

This project is perfect for the beginner who wants to make a piece that looks advanced. Connect the shaped punched tiles to create a bracelet that hugs the wrist and then make a matching toggle clasp.

BEGINNER   PUNCH PATTERN 8   TEMPLATE CALHOUN TILES

PUNCH THE PATTERN

1 Per the instructions in Chapter 2, adhere a copy of the pattern from the back of the book to the 24-gauge copper metal sheet. Punch the pattern over the whole piece of copper and clean the metal with warm water to remove the used pattern.

CUT OUT THE BRACELET TILES AND CLASP PIECES

2 Adhere a copy of the tile template to the punched sheet. Cut out the bracelet tiles, the bar half of the toggle, and the large oval of the ring half of the clasp using the metal shears (**Figure 1**). Use the hole-punch pliers to punch out a hole in the center of the small oval of the ring half of the clasp, thread the saw blade through the hole, and secure it in the frame of the jeweler's saw (**Figure 2**). Saw out the center oval per the instructions in Chapter 3.

FLATTEN THE TILES AND CLASP PIECES

3 After you've cut your tiles and clasp pieces, they will be warped. To flatten them, use the dead-blow mallet and strike them flat against the bench block. To smooth sharp metal edges, start by filing them with a metal file. If you need to file away a lot of excess material, choose a coarser file; if you just need to smooth a rough edge, choose a finer file. If you want to make your edges even smoother after you have filed them, sand them down with fine-grit sandpaper.

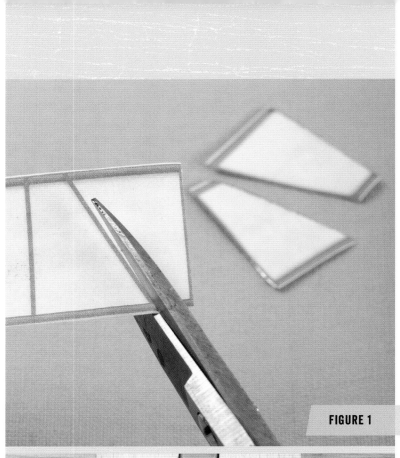

FIGURE 1

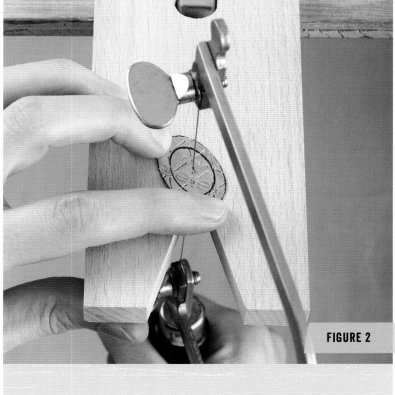

FIGURE 2

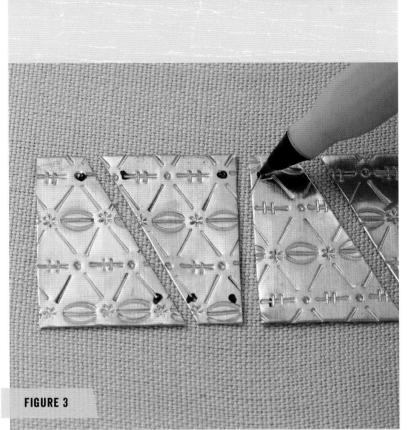

FIGURE 3

MAKE THE HOLES FOR THE JUMP RINGS

4 Arrange the tile pieces as they will be in the finished bracelet. Make a mark in the four corners of each tile (except the first and last, which need only two marks along their diagonal edge), ¼" (6 mm) from the exterior edge and ¹⁄₁₆" (2 mm) from the interior edge (**Figure 3**). Punch a hole through each mark with the hole-punch pliers.

SHAPE THE TILES

5 Start shaping the tiles using nylon ring-bending pliers. Start at one end of each tile and lightly tap the pliers all the way up to the other end (**Figure 4**). Because doing so will create a steep curve in the metal pieces, place the tiles on your bench block and press down on them gently to flatten them a bit.

PATINA THE TILES

6 Use liver of sulfur to antique your tiles and then rub with steel wool to remove the patina from the top surface. Arrange the tiles as they will be in the finished bracelet again, using the oval jump rings to attach them to each other.

ATTACH THE CLASP

8 Use the hole-punch pliers to punch two centered holes in the straight edge (outside edge) of the first tile, ¹⁄₁₆" (2 mm) from the edge. Punch two holes in the center of one of the long sides of the oval toggle loop, making sure they line up with the holes you just punched in the first tile. Connect the toggle ring to the first bracelet tile with two round jump rings.

9 Use the hole-punch pliers to punch one centered hole in the straight edge (outside edge) of the last tile, ¹⁄₃₂" (1 mm) away from the edge. Punch a hole in the center of the bar half of the clasp. Use one round jump ring to attach another jump ring to the last bracelet tile. Use another jump ring to attach the previous jump ring to the bar half of the clasp.

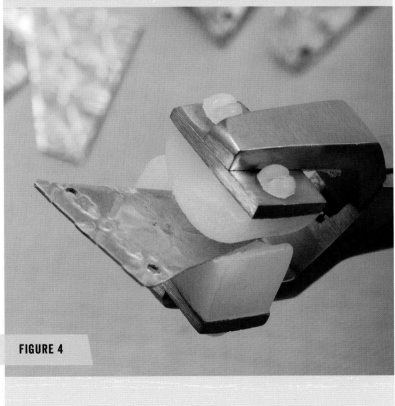

FIGURE 4

MATERIALS

3½" × 1½" (9 × 3.8 cm) piece of 22-gauge brass sheet

5" (12.5 cm) of 20-gauge sterling silver wire

TOOLS

Glue stick

Brass mallet

Bench block

Metal shears

Fine-point permanent marker

Metal file, medium to fine coarseness #2–#5

Fine-grit sandpaper

Dead-blow mallet (plastic, rubber, or urethane)

1⅛" (2.8 cm) diameter steel cylinder (I used a punch from my dapping set)

Sandbag

Large wrap-and-tap pliers

1.25 mm hole-punch pliers

Flush cutters

Chain-nose pliers

Round-nose pliers

Flat-nose pliers

Medium wrap-and-tap pliers

PUNCHES

Asterisk

Slash

Small Curve—Parenthesis

TECHNIQUES

Punching

Cutting

Shaping

Wrapped loops (see Techniques)

TAMARAC HOOP
EARRINGS

I love wearing hoop earrings. Something about them is feminine and fun, and the punched pattern keeps them from being too cutesy. The best part is that they're super easy to make.

BEGINNER   PUNCH PATTERN 5   TEMPLATE TAMARAC HOOPS

PUNCH THE PATTERN

1 Per the instructions in Chapter 2, adhere a copy of the pattern from the back of the book to the 22-gauge sheet metal. Punch the pattern over the whole piece of brass and clean the metal with warm water to remove the used pattern.

CUT THE HOOP PIECES

2 Adhere two copies of the hoop template to your punched sheet and cut them out using the metal shears. Clean the pieces with warm water to remove the used pattern (**Figure 1**). To smooth sharp metal edges, start by filing them with a metal file. If you need to file away a lot of excess material, choose a coarser file; if you just need to smooth a rough edge, choose a finer file. If you want to make your edges even smoother after you have filed them, sand them down with fine-grit sandpaper.

SHAPE THE HOOPS

3 Bend each hoop piece around the 1⅛" (2.8 cm) cylinder and lay it on the sandbag. Lightly hammer each piece all the way around with the dead-blow mallet and manipulate it with your hands until you create a nice round shape (**Figure 2**). If the hoop shape needs additional refining, use the large wrap-and-tap pliers.

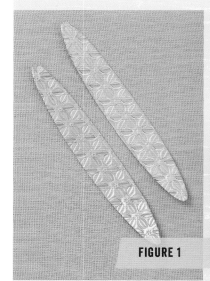

FIGURE 1

FIGURE 2

FIGURE 3

FIGURE 5

FIGURE 4

FIGURE 6

FIGURE 7

FORM THE EAR WIRE PADDLES

Using the flat-nose pliers, bend the last ⅕"–⅛" (about 4–5 mm) of both ends of each hoop shape outwards (as close to 90 degrees as possible) to create a paddle for the ear wire to attach to. Use the hole-punch pliers to punch a hole in the center of each paddle (**Figure 3**).

MAKE THE EAR WIRES

5 Cut a 2½" (6.5 cm) piece of 20-gauge wire and use the chain-nose pliers to make a 90-degree bend 1" (2.5 cm) from one end (**Figure 4**). Grasp the shorter side of the wire next to the bend with the round-nose pliers and create a loop. Thread the loop through the hole in one paddle on one hoop (**Figure 5**). Form a wrapped loop (see Techniques).

6 Using the largest barrel (10 mm) of the medium wrap-and-tap pliers, shape the ear wire into a soft arch shape (**Figure 6**). Bend the last ¼" (6 mm) of the ear wire outward 90 degrees (**Figure 7**). Manipulate the arch of the ear wire so that the wire end lines up with the hole in the other paddle. If the end of the wire is sharp, gently file it smooth.

7 Repeat Steps 5 and 6 to make the other earring.

CONSISTENT LOOPS

Using a fine-tip permanent marker, make a mark on the jaws of your round-nose pliers ⅛" (3 mm) from the tip. This will ensure that your wire loops will be the same size on both earrings.

MATERIALS

4" × 3½" (10 × 9 cm) piece of 24-gauge silver-filled sheet

4 sterling silver 1.3 mm nail-head rivets

1" (2.5 cm) of ³⁄₃₂" (2.5 mm) sterling silver tubing ⅝" × ⅜" (16 × 10 mm)

1 sterling silver ⅝" × ⅜" (16 × 10 mm) S-clasp (This S-clasp needs to have a section in the center that's large enough to punch a 1.5 mm hole into.)

122 teal 2 × 3mm tube beads

40 aqua 3 × 3mm tube beads

60 light blue 4 × 5mm ribbed barrel beads

195 opaque green 2 × 5mm four-petal flower spacer beads

1 gram of size 11° brass-colored seed beads

2 grams of size 11° matte silver seed beads

2 grams of size 11° dark red seed beads

3 sterling silver 18-gauge 5mm ID jump rings

2 sterling silver 10 × 15mm cones

10 sterling silver 2mm crimp beads

80" (2 m) of .014 beading wire

4" (10 cm) of 22-gauge sterling silver wire

TOOLS

Ruler

Fine-point permanent marker

Metal shears

Glue stick

Brass mallet

Bench block

Chasing hammer

Dead-blow mallet (plastic, rubber or urethane)

Metal file, medium to fine coarseness #2–#5

Fine-grit sandpaper

1.5 mm hole-punch pliers

Riveting hammer

Screw-down hole punch

Flaring tool (period stamp)

CONTINUED ON NEXT PAGE »

JOSEPHINE CRESCENT NECKLACE

This necklace is truly unique. The crescent shape repeats throughout the necklace to create a balanced design, with multiple strands of African trade beads to give the necklace a rich look. The hidden clasp is the icing on the cake. You'll love wearing this beautiful and comfortable design.

ADVANCED PUNCH PATTERN 5 TEMPLATE **JOSEPHINE CRESCENT**

TOOLS (CONTINUED)

Round needle file

Tube-cutting jig

Jeweler's saw, saw blades, and cut
   lubricant

Bench pin and clamp

Silver Black or liver of sulfur

Pro Polish Pad

Flush cutters

Round-nose pliers

Chain-nose pliers

Flat-nose pliers

PUNCHES

Asterisk

Slash

Small Curve—Parenthesis

TECHNIQUES

Punching

Texturing

Cutting

Riveting

Wrapped loops, page 120

Stringing

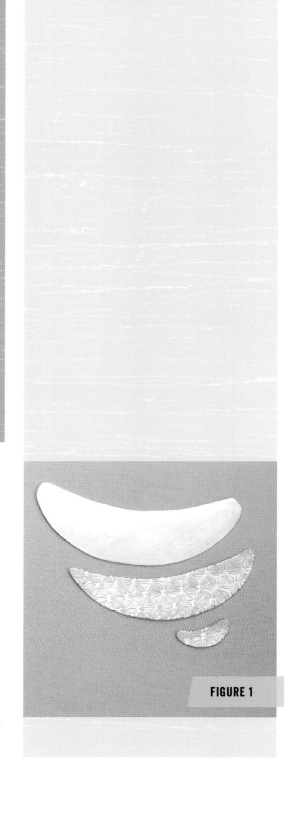

FIGURE 1

PREPARE THE METAL SHEET

1 Use the ruler and marker to draw a line dividing the silver-filled
sheet into one 4" × 2" (10 × 5 cm) piece and one 4" × 1½" (10 ×
3.8 cm) piece. Use the metal shears to cut along the marked line,
separating the two pieces.

PUNCH THE PATTERN

2 Per the instructions in Chapter 2, adhere a copy of the pattern
from the back of the book to the 4" × 1½" (10 × 3.8 cm) piece
of 24-gauge silver-filled metal sheet. Punch the pattern over the
whole piece of silver and then clean the metal with warm water to
remove the used pattern.

CUT OUT THE CRESCENT SHAPES

3 Adhere copies of the small and medium crescent templates from
the back of the book to your punched sheet and a copy of the large
crescent template to the plain sheet. Cut out the three crescents
using metal shears (**Figure 1**).

FIGURE 2

FIGURE 3

FIGURE 4

FIGURE 5

HAMMER TEXTURE ONTO THE LARGE CRESCENT

4 Texture the large crescent by placing it on the bench block and hammering it with the rounded head of the chasing hammer (**Figure 2**). Texture the whole surface, including the exposed edges, to soften them. Use a dead-blow mallet to flatten this piece against the bench block after you've textured it. To smooth sharp metal edges, start by filing them with a metal file. If you need to file away a lot of excess material, choose a coarser file; if you just need to smooth a rough edge, choose a finer file. If you want to make your edges even smoother after you've filed them, sand them down with fine-grit sandpaper.

RIVET THE CRESCENT PIECES TOGETHER

5 Using the photograph as a guide, make a mark with the fine-point permanent marker in each point and at the bottom of the medium crescent where you want your rivets to be. Use the hole-punch pliers to punch a hole through each mark.

6 Center the medium crescent on top of the large crescent piece. Using the tip of the fine-point permanent marker, make a mark through one hole in the medium crescent onto the large crescent piece below (**Figure 3**). Remove the medium crescent and punch a hole through the mark on the large crescent with the hole-punch pliers. Place the medium crescent back on top of the large crescent and align their holes.

7 Insert one nail-head rivet through the aligned holes, passing it through the stacked crescents from front to back (**Figure 4**). Rivet the nail-head rivet per the instructions in Chapter 3 (**Figure 5**). Rivet the two remaining rivets: align their placement, punch the hole by passing the punch through the top layer and down into the bottom layer, and flare the rivet.

ADD THE TUBE RIVETS

8 Once the medium crescent has been riveted in place, create a 2.3 mm hole at both points of the large crescent, using the large end of the screw-down hole punch. Use the round needle file to widen the holes until the 2.5 mm tubing just fits through it. Use the tube cutting jig and the jeweler's saw to cut two ⅙"–⅕" (4–5 mm) lengths of tubing for the tube rivets. One at a time, insert the tube rivets into the 2.3 mm holes and rivet them in place per the instructions in Chapter 3 (**Figure 6**).

ADD PATINA TO THE CRESCENT PIECES

9 Use liver of sulfur, Silver Black, or permanent marker to add patina to the riveted crescents and small stamped crescent. Polish and buff the top surface of the metal using a Pro Polish Pad.

MAKE THE CLASP

10 Using the hole-punch pliers, punch a hole through the center of the S-clasp. Insert a nail-head rivet through the smallest crescent and the hole in the S-clasp (**Figure 7**) and rivet them together per the instructions in Chapter 3.

STRING THE BEADS

11 Cut the 22-gauge wire in half and use each half to form a wrapped loop (**Figure 8**). Cut the beading wire into five 16" (40.5 cm) pieces.

12 Use one piece of beading wire to string one crimp bead and one of the wrapped loops. Pass back through the crimp bead and flatten it with a pair of flat- or chain-nose pliers (**Figure 9**). String [one brass-colored seed bead and one teal tube bead] forty times, and [one flower spacer bead and one dark red seed bead] sixty-five times. String one crimp bead and the

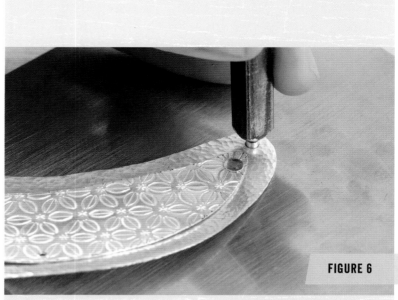

FIGURE 6

FIGURE 7

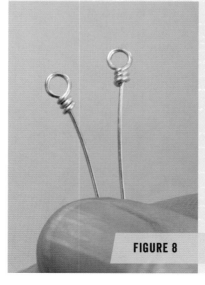

FIGURE 8

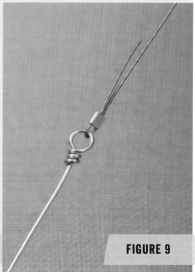

FIGURE 9

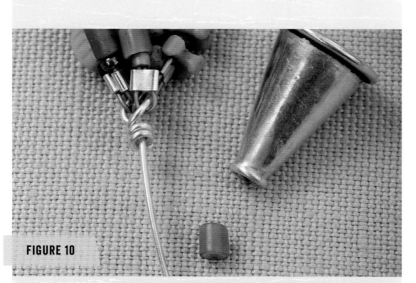

FIGURE 10

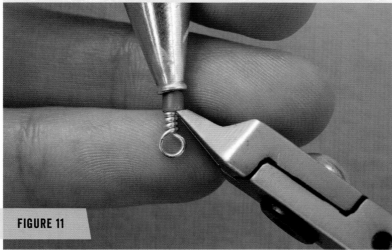

FIGURE 11

FIGURE 12

other wrapped loop. Pass back through the crimp bead and flatten. (African trade beads like the ones in this necklace tend to vary in size, so make sure that the rest of your beaded strands are about the same length as the first one before you crimp them.)

13 Repeat Step 12, this time stringing [one silver seed bead and one light blue barrel bead] thirty times, and [one dark red seed bead and one teal tube bead] forty times. Repeat Step 12, this time stringing [one dark red seed bead and one teal tube] forty times, and [one flower spacer bead and one silver seed bead} sixty-five times. Repeat Step 12, this time stringing [one silver seed bead and one flower spacer bead] sixty-five times, and [one light blue barrel bead and one dark red seed bead] thirty times. Repeat Step 12, this time stringing [one dark red seed bead and one aqua tube bead] forty times, and [one brass-colored seed bead and one teal tube bead] forty times.

14 Use the wire tail of one of the wrapped loops to string one cone (wide end first) and one teal tube bead (**Figure 10**). Form another wrapped loop and trim the wire (**Figure 11**). Repeat, using the tail of the other wrapped loop.

CONNECT YOUR COMPONENTS

15 Use one jump ring to connect one of the tube rivets in the crescent centerpiece to one of the previous wrapped loops. Attach another jump ring to the tube rivet on the other side of the centerpiece. Use the last jump ring to connect the other wrapped loop to a loop of the S-clasp (**Figure 12**). Bend the other loop of the S-clasp away from the small crescent so that it can be slipped over the free jump ring on the centerpiece to clasp the necklace.

MATERIALS

3" × 3" (7.5 × 7.5 cm) piece of 24-gauge copper sheet

12" (30.5 cm) of 1.5 mm red leather cord

11 copper 18-gauge 3.5mm ID jump rings

1 copper 18 × 9mm lobster clasp

2 copper 4 × 10mm leather crimp ends

TOOLS

Glue stick

Brass mallet

Bench block

Plastic oval template

Fine-point permanent marker

Metal shears

Metal file, medium to fine coarseness #2–#5

1.25 mm hole-punch pliers

Liver of sulfur

#0000 steel wool

Chain-nose pliers

Flat-nose pliers

Scissors

Hypo cement glue

PUNCHES

4 Petal—Cross Star

Period

Slash

Thin Arch

TECHNIQUES

Punching

Cutting

Hole punching

Knotting

WAVERLY NECKLACE

This design uses oval shapes, jump rings, and leather to create a necklace with plenty of movement. Feel free to switch up the shapes to create a different look. Part of the beauty of this piece is that the ovals get larger toward the center, but that doesn't have to be the case. Experiment with different shapes and have fun.

BEGINNER　　　　　　　　　　　**PUNCH PATTERN 2**

PUNCH THE PATTERN

1 Per the instructions in Chapter 2, adhere a copy of the pattern from the back of the book to the 24-gauge sheet metal. Punch the pattern over the whole piece of copper and clean the metal with warm water to remove the used pattern.

TRACE AND CUT YOUR SHAPE

2 Trace nine graduated ovals (one 1¾" × 7½" [30 × 19 mm] oval, two 10⅝" × 6¾" [27 × 17 mm] ovals, two 9¾" × 6¼" [25 × 16 mm] ovals, two 8¼" × 5½" [21 × 14 mm] ovals, and two 7½" × 4¾" [19 × 12 mm] ovals) onto the punched sheet using the plastic template. Cut out the shapes using the metal shears. To smooth sharp metal edges, start by filing them with a metal file. If you need to file away a lot of excess material, choose a coarser file; if you just need to smooth a rough edge, choose a finer file. If you want to make your edges even smoother after you have filed them, sand them down with fine-grit sandpaper.

MAKE THE HOLES FOR THE JUMP RINGS

3 Arrange the pieces in graduated order, with the largest oval in the center and the smallest ovals on either end. Make marks with the fine-point permanent marker where the holes for the jump rings will go, about 1⁄16" (2mm) from the edge (**Figure 1**). Punch a hole through each of the marks with the hole-punch pliers.

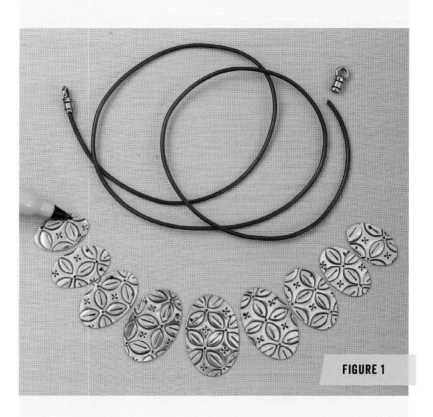

FIGURE 1

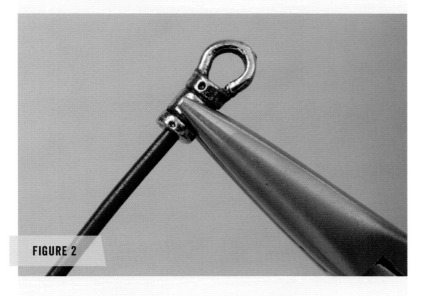

FIGURE 2

ADDING PATINA

4 Using liver of sulfur or the permanent marker, darken the punched impressions. Remove excess patina from the surface of the metal with the steel wool.

CONNECTING COMPONENTS

5 Use jump rings to attach all nine ovals together and attach jump rings to the outer holes on the first and last oval to later be used to attach the leather cord.

ADD THE LEATHER AND CLASP

6 Use the scissors to cut the leather in half. Use one half to tie an overhand knot in the leather through one of the free jump rings attached the outermost ovals. Dab the end of the leather with glue, thread the end through the crimp end, and crimp. Thread the other end of the leather piece into one crimp end and crimp with chain-nose pliers (**Figure 2**). Repeat on the other end of the necklace. Use the final jump ring to attach the lobster clasp to the loop of one crimp end.

MATERIALS

Piece of 24-gauge brass sheet (required dimension determined in Step 1)

1³⁄₈" × ¹⁵⁄₁₆" (3.5 × 2.3 cm) oval copper blank

5 copper nail-head rivets, 1.3 mm × ¼" (6 mm) long

TOOLS

Ruler

Fine-point permanent marker

Metal shears

Brass mallet

Bench block

Metal file, medium to fine coarseness #2–#5

Fine-grit sandpaper

1.5 mm hole-punch pliers

Riveting hammer

Bench block

Nylon ring-bending pliers

Steel ring mandrel

Flush cutters

Sandbag

Dead-blow mallet (plastic, rubber, or urethane)

Silver Black

Pro Polish Pad

Riveting tiles

PUNCHES

Plain Heart

Period

"V"

Crescent Burst

TECHNIQUES

Freehand punching

Shaping

Riveting

Cutting

Patinating

VERMILION RING

This rustic statement ring is the all-in-one style for the cowgirl and cowboy in all of us. The inspiration for this design came after a trip to Phoenix in 2011, where I spent a couple of days treasure hunting in the local antiques shops for jewelry.

BEGINNER   PUNCH PATTERN **FREEHAND**

DETERMINE YOUR RING-BAND BLANK LENGTH AND CUT OUT YOUR RING BAND

1   The first step is to find the circumference of the ring size you would like to make. The second step is finding the thickness of the metal you'll be using for the ring band. Multiply the thickness of the metal by three, and add it to the circumference. This is the length you will cut your ring-band blank to be to make the exact size you want.

To make a size 6 ring with 24-gauge sheet metal (which is .5 mm in thickness): 51.9 mm (size 6) + = 1.5 mm (.5 mm is the thickness of the metal x 3) = 53.4 mm.

Note: This equation is meant to be used with 24-gauge sheet metal. If you use a different gauge for your ring band, refer to page 121 to make your calculations.

2   Use the ruler and fine-point permanent marker to draw the dimensions that you found in Step 1 onto the brass sheet metal. Cut out your ring blank using the metal shears.

PUNCH THE PATTERN

3   Punch your freehand pattern into the ring band and copper oval. Freehand stamping can be done "off the cuff," or you can use the fine-tip permanent marker to plot out your design (**Figure 1**). To smooth sharp metal edges, start by filing them with a metal file. If you need to file away a lot of excess material, choose a coarser file; if you just need to smooth a rough edge, choose a finer file. If you want to make your edges even smoother, sand them down with fine-grit sandpaper.

RIVET THE PIECES TOGETHER

4   Use the hole-punch pliers to punch the holes for the nail-head rivets in the copper oval. Your rivets should be far enough toward the middle of the copper ovals that they will not flare over the edges. In the sample shown, I placed two holes on either side of the long sides of the oval.

CIRCUMFERENCE (MM)	INTERNATIONAL RING SIZE
46.8	4
48.0	4.5
49.3	5
50.6	5.5
51.9	6
53.1	6.5
54.4	7
55.7	7.5
57.0	8
58.3	8.5
59.5	9
60.8	9.5
62.1	10
63.4	10.5
64.6	11
65.9	11.5
67.2	12

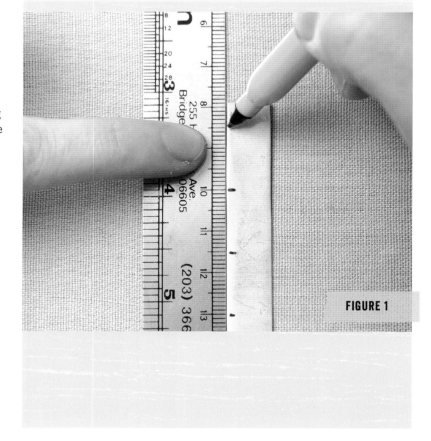

FIGURE 1

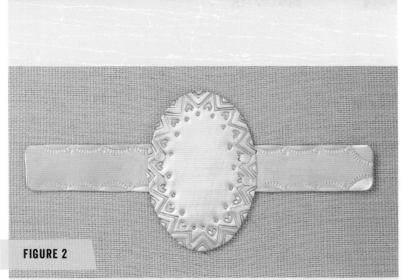

FIGURE 2

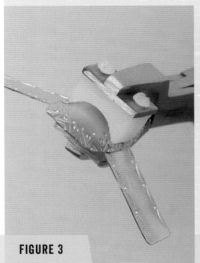

FIGURE 3

FIGURE 4

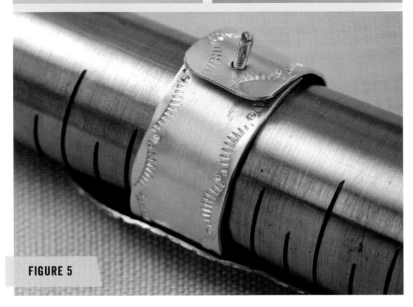

FIGURE 5

5 Center the copper oval on top of the brass band and use the holes you punched in Step 4 as a guideline to mark where one of the rivet holes needs to be on the ring band. Punch a hole through the mark.

6 Thread the nail-head rivet through the hole on both ring pieces from the back side of the band. Rivet all the nail-head rivets per the instructions in Chapter 3 (**Figure 2**). Rivet the remaining three rivets one by one: pass the hole-punch pliers through the hole in the copper oval and punch the brass ring band, then rivet using a nail-head rivet.

SHAPE THE RING

7 Use the nylon ring-bending pliers to shape your ring into a circle by starting in the middle of the ring (**Figure 3**) and working your way to the ends. The last 7 mm of both ends of the ring band should overlap.

RIVET THE ENDS OF THE BAND TOGETHER

8 To create the hole for the rivet on the back side of the ring, punch a hole through both layers of metal where they overlap using the hole-punch pliers (**Figure 4**). Then, insert the final nail-head rivet through the holes from the inside of the ring. Slide the ring onto the steel ring mandrel (**Figure 5**). Trim the nail-head rivet using the flush cutters, leaving 2 mm of length visible above the metal sheet. Place the ring mandrel onto the sandbag and finish the rivet. If your ring band is not round at this point, lightly tap it with a dead-blow mallet before taking it off the steel ring mandrel.

PATINA AND POLISH

9 Using Silver Black or the permanent marker, apply a dark patina over the stamped copper oval. Buff the excess patina away with a Pro Polish Pad until the metal shines.

MATERIALS

4 sterling silver ³⁄₁₆" (5 mm) 24-gauge circular blanks

4 sterling silver ¼" (6 mm) 24-gauge circular blanks

4 sterling silver ⁵⁄₁₆" (8 mm) 24-gauge circular blanks

4 sterling silver ³⁄₈" (1 cm) 24-gauge circular blanks

4 sterling silver ⁷⁄₁₆" (11 mm) 24-gauge circular blanks

10 sterling silver 18-gauge 3.5mm ID jump rings

1 pair of sterling silver ear wires

TOOLS

Fine-point permanent marker

Brass mallet

Bench block

Dapping set

1.25 mm hole-punch pliers

Liver of sulfur or Silver Black

Pro Polish Pad

Chain-nose pliers

Flat-nose pliers

PUNCHES

Asterisk

Medium Tripod

Period

Short Dash

"V"

TECHNIQUES

Freehand punching

Dapping

Patinating

Hole punching

CASCADE CLUSTER EARRINGS

These cascading earrings are a wonderful way to show off your punched pattern. This design has a lot of possibilities: add more sizes or add twice the quantity to each earring and make a longer version.

BEGINNER   **PUNCH PATTERN FREEHAND**

For this project, you may use premade blanks or you can cut your own discs using a disc cutter. To create these clusters, you'll combine five different sizes of discs.

PUNCH YOUR PATTERN

1   Use the fine-point permanent marker to plot out a freehand design on each blank. Punch your pattern onto all the discs.

DAP THE DISCS

2   Use the dapping set to dap the punched discs facedown per the instructions on page 31. Strike the dap softly and carefully so as not to damage the punched pattern created on the front side of each circle.

MAKE THE HOLES IN THE DISCS

3   Use the fine-point permanent marker to mark where you would like to punch the hole for the jump rings in each disc, about $\frac{1}{16}$" (2 mm) from the edge. Punch the holes with the hole-punch pliers.

PATINA AND POLISH

4   Using liver of sulfur, Silver Black, or permanent marker, apply a dark patina over all the domed surface of the discs. Buff the excess patina away with the Pro Polish Pad until surface is shiny.

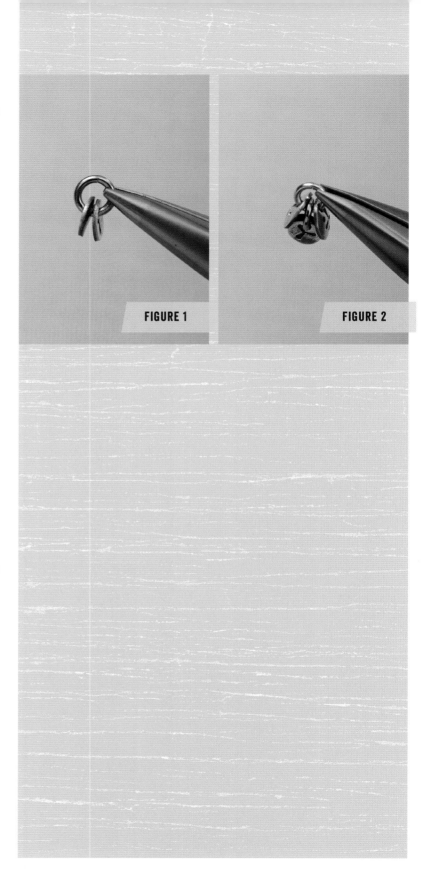

FIGURE 1

FIGURE 2

CONNECT THE CLUSTERS TOGETHER

5 Use one jump ring to attach two $^3/_{16}$"
(5 mm) discs, stamped sides facing out
(**Figure 1**). Use another jump ring to attach two $^1/_4$" (6 mm) discs (stamped sides
facing out) to the previous jump ring
(**Figure 2**). Continue in this fashion to
attach two $^5/_{16}$" (8 mm) discs, two $^3/_8$"
(1 cm) discs, and two $^7/_{16}$" (11 mm) discs
to the cluster.

FINISH THE EARRINGS

6 Attach an ear wire to the last jump ring
added in Step 5 by opening and closing
its loop as you would a jump ring. Repeat
Steps 5 and 6 to create the second earring.

CHARM MATERIALS

1" × 1" (2.5 × 2.5 cm) piece of 24-gauge copper sheet

1" × 1" (2.5 × 2.5 cm) piece of 24-gauge silver-filled sheet

1" × 1" (2.5 × 2.5 cm) piece of 24-gauge brass sheet

5 brass 12-gauge 10mm OD jump rings

7" (18 cm) of 6 × 8 mm antique brass flat cable chain

Copper 17 × 9mm lobster clasp

PENDANT MATERIALS

6" (15 cm) piece of 22-gauge wire

8' (2.4 m) of beading wire

Two 18" (45.5 cm) strands of African Silver Metal Seed Beads, 11°

Two 18" (45.5 cm) strands of African Brass Metal Seed Beads, 11°

Sterling silver bead caps with a 6 mm opening

Sterling silver leaves hook-and-eye clasp

TOOLS

Glue stick

Brass mallet

Bench block

Plastic templates of your choice

Fine-point permanent marker

Metal shears

Metal file, medium to fine coarseness #2–#5

Fine-grit sandpaper

Screw-down hole punch

Pro Polish Pad

Chain-nose pliers

Flat-nose pliers

Wire cutters

Round-nose pliers

Jeweler's saw, saw blades, and cut lubricant

Bench pin with clamp

CONTINUED ON NEXT PAGE »

LAKE SUPERIOR CHARMS & PENDANT

Charms are a great way to add flair to a piece of jewelry. Switch up the punched pattern, metal color, and charm shape to create a different look and feel every time. The charms and pendant featured here showcase the punched pattern in a very simple design. Beginners will find this pendant a snap to make using just a few basic jewelry tools.

■■ INTERMEDIATE
PUNCH PATTERNS 2 (COPPER CHARM) & 5 (SILVER AND BRASS CHARMS)

(CONTINUED)

PUNCHES

Copper charm:

4 Petal—
    Cross Star

Period

Thin Arch

Slash

Silver-Filled Charm:

Asterisk: 1.6 mm

Slash

Small Curve—
    Parenthesis

Brass Charm:

Asterisk

Slash

Small Curve—
    Parenthesis

Brass Pendant:

Period

Slash

Small Curve—
    Parenthesis

TECHNIQUES

Punching

Cutting or sawing

Patinating

PUNCH THE PATTERN

1   Per the instructions in Chapter 2, adhere a copy of the pattern from the back of the book to the appropriate piece of 24-gauge sheet metal. Punch the pattern over the entire piece and clean the metal with warm water to remove the used pattern.

TRACE AND CUT YOUR SHAPE

2   Trace the shapes in the plastic template onto your sheet metal with a fine-point permanent marker. Cut out your charm piece using the metal shears. To smooth sharp metal edges, start by filing them with a metal file. If you need to file away a lot of excess material, choose a coarser file; if you just need to smooth a rough edge, choose a finer file. If you want to make your edges even smoother after you have filed them, sand them down with fine-grit sandpaper.

MAKE THE HOLE FOR THE JUMP RING

3   Make a mark on each charm/pendant with the fine-point permanent marker where the hole needs to be punched, about 2 mm from the edge. Punch 2.3 mm holes through each mark with the large end of the screw-down hole punch.

GET SHAPELY

If you choose a particularly intricate template shape or are working with a thick sheet of metal, you may choose to use the jeweler's saw instead of metal shears. See Chapter 3 for more information about using a jeweler's saw.

DARKEN THE IMPRESSIONS

4 Use the permanent marker to darken the punched impressions in the charms and pendant. Remove excess patina from the surface of the metal with the Pro Polish Pad.

CONNECT THE BRACELET COMPONENTS

5 Attach one jump ring to each of the stamped charms. Use another jump ring to attach the three previous jump rings to the end of the cable chain. Attach the lobster clasp to the other end of the chain with a jump ring.

STRING THE NECKLACE

6 Create the pendant following Steps 1–4.

7 Cut the 6" (15 cm) piece of 22-gauge wire in half and use the end of each half to form a wrapped loop. Use 20" (51 cm) of beading wire to string one crimp bead and one of the wrapped loops. Pass a short tail back through the crimp bead and flatten it with a pair of chain- or flat-nose pliers (see Techniques). String 16" (40.5 cm) of silver beads, another crimp bead, and the other wrapped loop. Pass back through the crimp bead and flatten it. Repeat entire step three more times to string another strand of silver beads and two strands of brass beads.

8 Use the wire tail on one of the wrapped loops to string one cone (wide end first). Form a wrapped loop that attaches to one half of the clasp. Repeat using the other wire tail, another cone, and the other half of the clasp. Use a jump ring to attach the stamped pendant to all four beaded strands.

MATERIALS

5 brass ½" (1.3 cm) circular blanks

1 brass ¾" (2 cm) circular blank

1 copper ½" (1.3 cm) circular blank

2 copper ⅝" (1.5 cm) circular blanks

1 copper ½" (1.3 cm) circular blank

2 copper 1" (2.5 cm) circular blanks

1½" × 1" (3.8 × 2.5 cm) piece of 24-gauge brass sheet

3" × 3" (7.5 × 7.5 cm) piece of 24-gauge copper sheet

5" × 1" (12.5 × 2.5 cm) scalloped brass necklace blank

34 garnet 8mm rounds

2' (61 cm) of .019 beading wire

4 copper 2mm crimp tubes

4 copper 3mm crimp covers

1 gram of size 11° brown seed beads

1 antique brass lobster clasp

Nail-head rivets

TOOLS

Fine-point permanent marker

Metal shears

Metal file, medium to fine coarseness #2–#5

Fine-grit sandpaper

Sandpaper

Brass mallet

Bench block

Dapping set

Dead-blow mallet (plastic, rubber, or urethane)

#0000 steel wool

1.5 mm hole-punch pliers

Electric or manual drill

Drill bit 1.5 mm

Flush cutters

Riveting hammer

Chain-nose pliers

CONTINUED ON NEXT PAGE »

HARRIET BOUQUET NECKLACE

The Harriet Bouquet Necklace reminds me of a corsage; the punching on this design is reminiscent of embroidery. In this design, I used design stamps, letters, and numbers from a letter set. This gave me more options for making the blanks look like flowers.

■■■ **ADVANCED**
PUNCH PATTERN FREEHAND   **TEMPLATE HARRIET BOUQUET**

(CONTINUED)

PUNCHES	TECHNIQUES
Letter U, Block font: 6.4 mm and 2.5 mm	Freehand punching
Letter O: 2.5 mm	Cutting
Period	Riveting
Asterisk	Shaping
Circle Set: 2 mm, 4 mm and 6 mm	Stringing
Short Dash	Hole punching
Slash	Drilling

MAKE THE LEAVES

1   Using the fine-point permanent marker, freehand draw a 1" × ⅝" (2.5 × 1.5 cm) leaf onto the 24-gauge brass sheet metal and two 1" × ½" (2.5 × 1.3 cm) leaves and a ¾" × ⅜" (2 × 1 cm) leaf onto the 24-gauge copper sheet metal (or use the leaf template at the back of the book). Cut out the leaf shapes with the metal shears. To smooth sharp metal edges, start by filing them with a metal file. If you need to file away a lot of excess material, choose a coarser file; if you just need to smooth a rough edge, choose a finer file. If you want to make your edges even smoother after you have filed them, sand them down with fine-grit sandpaper.

LAY OUT YOUR DESIGN

2   Arrange the circle blanks on the scalloped necklace blank. Play with different arrangements and placements. Make a sketch or take a picture of your arrangement to reference as you construct your necklace.

PUNCH THE BLANKS

3   Freehand stamp the designs into the circle blanks and leaf blanks you created. I recommend starting to stamp in the center of each circle and working your way out. This is an easy way to build on a central design.

SHAPE THE FLOWERS

4   Lay out the blanks onto the necklace piece as in Step 2. Decide which flowers will have three-dimensional shaping to them and which will lie flat against the necklace piece. Dap the flowers you would like to have raised off the surface per the instructions in Chapter 3.

FIGURE 1

FIGURE 2

DARKEN THE IMPRESSIONS

5 Use the permanent marker to darken the punched impressions. Remove excess patina from the surface of the metal with steel wool.

PUNCH THE RIVET HOLES IN THE FLOWERS AND LEAVES

6 Punch a hole at the center of each stamped circle and the tip of each leaf using the hole-punch pliers.

RIVET THE NECKLACE TOGETHER

7 Lay out the stamped leaves and the smallest stamped circles on your necklace blank and use the fine-point permanent marker to create a mark through each of their holes onto the scalloped necklace piece. The brass necklace piece that you're building on is very hard, so you'll need a drill or flex shaft to drill through it. Drill holes through each mark you just made. Rivet each blank and leaf down to the necklace piece using the nail-head riveting technique (**Figure 1**). Repeat this entire step to rivet the rest of the stamped circles onto the scalloped necklace blank (**Figure 2**).

STRING THE NECKLACE

8 Drill a hole through one tip of the scalloped base where it will attach to the neck strap. Use 12" (30.5 cm) of beading wire to string one crimp tube, eleven size 11° seed beads, and the hole you just made in the necklace base. Pass back through the tube, snug the seed bead loop, and crimp the crimp tube. Cover the crimp tube with one crimp cover. String seventeen garnet beads, one crimp tube, five seed beads, the clasp, and five more seed beads. Pass back through the crimp tube, snug the seed bead loop, crimp the tube, and cover with a crimp cover. Repeat entire step to string the other half of the necklace, omitting the clasp this time.

MATERIALS

14 sterling silver ⅝" (1.5 cm) circular blanks

12 sterling silver ½" (1.3 cm) circular blanks

32 sterling silver ⅜" (1 cm) circular blanks

29 graduated 10–20 × 7–16mm agate rondelles

30 sterling silver 3mm spacer beads

4' (1.2 m) of .019 beading wire

2 sterling silver 2mm crimp tubes

2 sterling silver 3mm crimp covers

1 sterling silver hook (18 × 10mm) and eye (13 × 8mm) clasp

TOOLS

1.5 mm hole-punch pliers

Clear plastic grid ruler

Fine-point permanent marker

Glue stick

Brass mallet

Bench block

Dapping set

Dead-blow mallet (plastic, rubber, or urethane)

Liver of sulfur

Pro Polish Pad

Crimping pliers

Wire cutters

Chain-nose pliers

PUNCHES

Plain Heart

Period

Short Dash

Slash

Small Curve—Parenthesis

TECHNIQUES

Punching

Stringing

Shaping

Patinating

TOTAL LENGTH

19½" (49.5 cm)

HALF-MOON BEAD CAPS

Punched-pattern bead caps add a lot of style to a simple strand of beads. I was inspired to create this design when I purchased a strand of large graduated stones that needed to be visually framed. For this project, you can use premade blanks or cut your own discs using a disc cutter.

■■■ ADVANCED   TEMPLATE HALF-MOON BEAD CAPS

For this design, I punched a freehand pattern. When you design a bead cap, it's helpful to start your pattern in the middle near the hole and work outward. This will create a more balanced design and will set you up for success! If you would like to create your own design on your bead caps, feel free to deviate from the pattern in the back of the book.

MAKE A HOLE IN THE BEAD CAPS

1   Begin by making a hole with the hole-punch pliers in the clear plastic grid ruler in the center of a large section of grid (**Figure 1**). This will be your handy way to find the center of your circle blanks. Lay each blank under the grid ruler, centering it so that the circle covers the same amount of grid all the way around (**Figure 2**). Place a mark through the hole in the grid ruler at the center of each blank with the fine-point permanent marker. Use the hole-punch pliers to punch a hole through each mark.

PUNCH YOUR BEAD CAPS

2   You can follow the punched pattern in the back of the book. Otherwise, the options are endless.

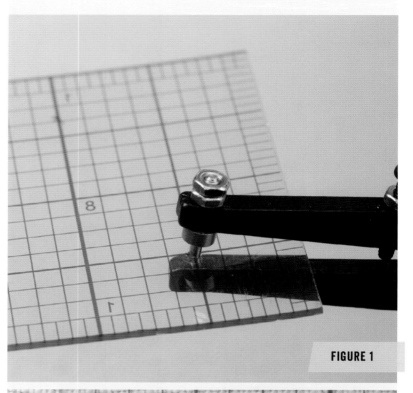

FIGURE 1

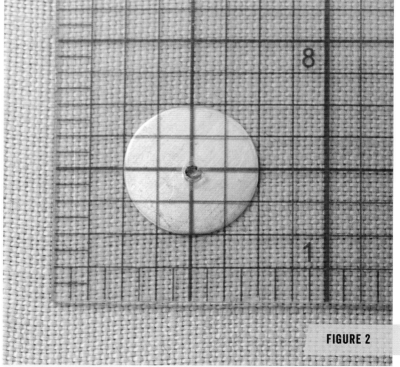

FIGURE 2

DAP YOUR BEAD CAPS

3 Dap your punched discs into domed bead caps per the instructions in Chapter 3. Dap all the discs facedown. Dapping may distort the center hole; if this happens, repunch the hole using the hole-punch pliers.

PATINA AND POLISH THE BEAD CAPS

4 Use liver of sulfur, Silver Black, or permanent marker to add patina to your bead caps. Rub each one with the Pro Polish Pad to remove the excess patina from the surface of the metal.

THREAD YOUR BEADS AND FINISH YOUR NECKLACE

5 Fold your beading wire in half (to double its strength). Use one end of your doubled wire to string one crimp tube and one half of the clasp. Pass back through the tube and crimp. Cover the crimp tube with one crimp cover. String [one spacer bead, one stamped bead cap, one agate rondelle, and one stamped bead cap] twenty-nine times, stringing the beads and bead caps in graduated order. String one spacer bead, one crimp tube, and the other half of the clasp. Pass back through the tube, crimp, and cover.

MATERIALS

2" × ¾" (5 × 2 cm) piece of 24-gauge silver-filled sheet for the turquoise pendant

2" × 1¼" (5 × 3.2 cm) piece of 24-gauge brass sheet

Large stone pendant, predrilled at one end (shown: ¾" × 2" [2 × 5 cm] turquoise pendant and 1⅜" × 2⅛" [3.4 × 5.2 cm] agate pendant

1" (2.5 cm) of 16-gauge brass wire

TOOLS

Glue stick

Brass mallet

Bench block

Paper

Scissors

Straight pin

Metal shears

Metal file, medium to fine coarseness #2–#5

Fine-grit sandpaper

Plastic bail template (optional)

Fine-point permanent marker

1.5 mm hole-punch pliers

Liver of sulfur

#0000 steel wool

Small metal mandrel

Flush cutters

Riveting hammer

PUNCHES

Silver-filled bail:

Crescent Burst

Period

Circle Set: 2 mm, 4 mm, and 6 mm

Elongated Teardrop

Thin Arch

Brass bail:

Period

Circle Set: 2 mm, 4 mm, 6 mm

Slash

TECHNIQUES

Punching

Cutting

Shaping

Wire riveting

BALSAM-WRAPPED BAILED STONE PENDANT

Give your natural stone pendants a truly unique hand-wrapped bail. Shape punched sheet metal or freehand punch your own design and secure with a wire rivet to make this striking pendant.

INTERMEDIATE

PUNCH PATTERN FREEHAND (SILVER-FILLED BAIL); 8 (BRASS BAIL)

PUNCH YOUR PATTERN

1   Per the instructions in Chapter 2, adhere a copy of the pattern to the 24-gauge metal sheet and punch the pattern over the whole piece of metal or freehand punch a design. Clean the metal with warm water to remove the used pattern.

2   Create your own paper bail template or use a plastic template.

OPTION 1:
MAKE YOUR OWN BAIL TEMPLATE

A   Use a piece of paper to build a model for your bail. Cut the paper to roughly the size you would like the finished bail to be and then wrap it around the top of your stone to represent the finished bail (**Figure 1A**). Make adjustments as you see fit. This may mean trimming the paper to make the paper template smaller or adding curves.

B   Once you have a shape and size you're happy with, wrap the paper template around the top of the stone piece, leaving space for the necklace strand or chain you plan to use to pass through the top portion. Using a straight pin, poke through the front of the paper, the predrilled hole in the stone, and the back of the paper. This will create even marks in your paper where the hole will need to be on the front and the back of the bail (**Figure 2**). Now you have a paper template to use when cutting out the sheet metal and placing holes for your rivet. If you would like to make this same bail again, make a photocopy of this template to save.

3   Adhere the template onto sheet metal using the glue stick. Cut out the shape using the metal shears. File and sand all edges smooth.

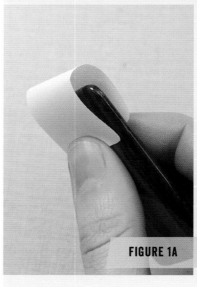

FIGURE 1A

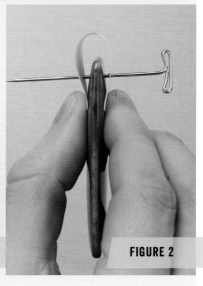

FIGURE 2

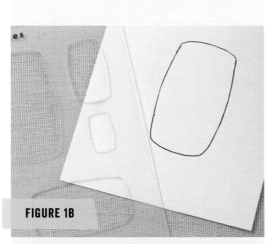

FIGURE 1B

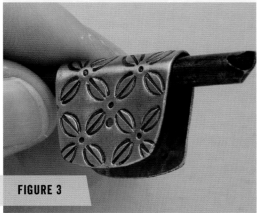

FIGURE 3

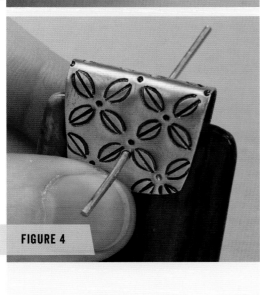

FIGURE 4

OPTION 2:
USE A PLASTIC BAIL TEMPLATE

A Trace the shape of the plastic bail template onto a piece of paper and cut it out with scissors (**Figure 1B**). Wrap the paper bail around the top of your pendant as described in the previous option and use a straight pin to poke through the front of the paper, the predrilled hole in the stone, and the back of the paper (**Figure 2**). Trace your paper bail shape onto punched sheet metal using the fine-point permanent marker. Using the metal shears cut out the shape. Use the holes in the paper template as your guide for placing the rivet holes. To smooth sharp metal edges, start by filing them with a metal file. If you need to file away a lot of excess material, choose a coarser file; if you just need to smooth a rough edge, choose a finer file. If you want to make your edges even smoother after you have filed them, sand them down with fine-grit sandpaper.

MAKE THE RIVET HOLES

3 Using the holes in the paper template as a guide, punch the holes in your bail using the hole-punch pliers.

DARKEN THE IMPRESSIONS

4 Using liver of sulfur or a permanent marker, darken the punched impressions. Remove excess patina from the surface of the metal with steel wool.

SHAPE THE BAIL

5 You'll want to find a round mandrel roughly the same thickness as your pendant. Pens and metal mandrels (I use a thin design stamp) work well for this step. Using your fingers, gently wrap the center of the flat bail piece around the mandrel, pressing the bail into a U shape (**Figure 3**). Place the bail over the top of your pendant to check that both of the holes in your bail are aligned with the hole drilled in the pendant. Make adjustments as needed.

RIVET THE BAIL ONTO THE TOP OF THE PENDANT

6 Cut a piece of 16-gauge wire longer than the total thickness of the pendant and the bail when assembled. Thread the wire through one side of the bail, the drilled hole in the pendant, and the other side of the bail and place the assembled pendant on the bench block (**Figure 4**). Use flush cutters to trim the riveting wire down so that just 1/16" (2 mm) still shows above the bail. Hold the main portion of the pendant off the side of the bench block, with the bail and the riveting wire resting firmly on the bench block. Rivet the bail using the "Tap and Flip" wire riveting method from Chapter 3 to rivet the bail onto the pendant. Be careful: when you rivet this pendant, it's important to rivet lightly to prevent the pendant from cracking.

MATERIALS

1¼" × 1 ¾" (3.2 × 4.5 cm) piece of 24-gauge brass sheet

2 antique silver ½" (1.3 cm) pre-made bezels with attached loop

1 antique silver ⅞" (2.2 cm) pre-made bezel with attached loop

7" (18 cm) of 6 × 8 mm antique silver oval chain

3 silver 12-gauge 10mm jump rings

1 black wood 20mm horn toggle clasp

1 pair of sterling silver ear wires

TOOLS

Glue stick

Brass mallet

Bench block

Dead-blow mallet

Disc cutter (or purchase circle blanks)

1 lb brass mallet or a household hammer

Dapping set

Fine-point permanent marker

#0000 steel wool

Jeweler's saw, saw blades, and cut lubricant

Bench pin and clamp

Pro Polish Pad

Nylon-coated chain-nose pliers

Chain-nose pliers

Flat-nose pliers

PUNCHES

Period

Slash

Small Curve—Parenthesis

TECHNIQUES

Punching

Sawing

Dapping

Disc cutting

Patinating

BIRCH-BEZELED TILE PENDANT & EARRINGS

Ready-made bezels create a beautiful frame for your punched work. I was using many different styles of bezels with images and resin a few years back. I had quite the collection and was excited when I came up with this alternative way to use them. These bezels can be found in a variety of metals; play with mixing metals to add contrast to your designs.

INTERMEDIATE   **PUNCH PATTERN 1**

PUNCH YOUR PATTERN

1 Per the instructions in Chapter 2, adhere a copy of the pattern from the back of the book to the 24-gauge sheet metal. Punch the pattern over the whole piece of brass and clean the metal with warm water to remove the used pattern.

CUT YOUR STAMPED DISC

2 Use a disc cutter to cut the discs the same size as the outside diameter of the bezel. To assist in this step, trace the bezel directly onto your punched sheet and use the marked circle as a guide to choose the right hole to use in your disc cutter. If you would like your punched piece to sit flat against the bottom of the bezel instead of doming, cut it to the dimensions of the inside of the bezel and skip Step 3.

DAP THE DISC

3 To add dimension to the punched piece, dap it to create a domed look. Place the disc pattern-down into the dapping set. Continue to increase the depth of the dome by shaping it with increasingly deeper wells in your dapping block until the piece fits snugly into the bezel. Be careful when dapping; dap lightly so as not to damage your punched pattern.

DARKEN THE IMPRESSIONS

4 Use the fine-point permanent marker to darken the punched impressions. Remove excess ink from the surface of the metal with steel wool.

FIGURE 1

FIGURE 2

FIGURE 3

MAKE THE SETTING TABS

5 To mount the punched piece into the bezel, you will need to create tabs in the sidewalls of the bezel. Use the fine-point permanent marker to mark where you want the tabs to be (**Figure 1**). Make no less than three tabs to hold your piece in place. This will ensure that your finished project will be secure. Using the jeweler's saw (per the instructions in Chapter 3), saw down to the base of the bezel on either side of each mark you created. Try to be consistent with the width of your tabs (**Figure 2**). Remove the excess ink with a Pro Polish Pad. Place each stamped circle into its bezel and push the tabs down over the piece using the nylon-coated chain-nose pliers to secure it in place (**Figure 3**).

ASSEMBLE

6 Use a jump ring to attach the large finished bezel to the chain. Attach half of the clasp to each end of the chain with jump rings to finish the bracelet. Attach each small bezel to an ear wire by opening and closing the loop of the earring as you would a jump ring (more on jump rings in the Techniques section).

MATERIALS

4" × 4¾" (10 × 12 cm) piece of 24-gauge copper sheet

10" (25.5 cm) of 20-gauge copper wire

TOOLS

Glue stick

Brass mallet

Bench block

Dead-blow mallet (plastic, rubber, or urethane)

Metal file, medium to fine coarseness #2–#5

Fine-grit sandpaper

Liver of sulfur

#0000 steel wool

Fine-point permanent marker

1.5 mm hole-punch pliers

Round-nose pliers

Chain-nose pliers

Flush cutters

PUNCHES

Period

Slash

Short Dash

Circle Set: 2 mm, 4 mm, and 6 mm

Small Curve—Parenthesis

TECHNIQUES

Punching

Freehand punching

Wrapped loops (see Techniques section)

Patinating

TO PURCHASE PATTERNS

Owlbert: sublimestitching.com/products/owlbert-pdf

Hello Banner from the Black Apple Sheet by Emily Martin: sublimestitching.com/products/the-black-apple-embroidery-patterns

HELLO OWL WALL PIECE

Using other patterns than the ones included in this book is a great way to expand on this technique. Embroidery patterns, clip-art pattern books, taking a picture of your favorite iron gate or tile floor can quickly be made into a pattern you can punch into sheet metal. For this project, I used an embroidery pattern I purchased as a PDF. I then made the image smaller to fit the size wall hanging I wanted to make.

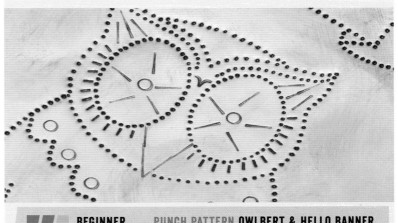

BEGINNER PUNCH PATTERN **OWLBERT & HELLO BANNER**
by Sublime Stitching

113

PUNCH THE PATTERN

1   Per the instructions in Chapter 2, adhere a copy of the embroidery pattern to the 24-gauge copper sheet (**Figure 1**). Punch the embroidery pattern into the copper and clean the metal with warm water to remove the used pattern. Use the small curve punch to stamp a freehand border all the way around the edge of copper sheet. The sheet may begin to warp as you are punching your pattern. Flatten the metal by tapping it with the dead-blow mallet. To smooth sharp metal edges, start by filing them with a metal file. If you need to file away a lot of excess material, choose a coarser file; if you just need to smooth a rough edge, choose a finer file. If you want to make your edges even smoother after you have filed them, sand them down with fine-grit sandpaper.

DARKEN THE IMPRESSIONS

2   Use the liver of sulfur or the permanent marker to darken the punched impressions. Remove excess patina from the surface of the metal with the steel wool.

MAKE THE HANGING WIRE PORTION

3   Place two marks on the top of the stamped sheet with the marker about ⁹⁄₁₆" (18 mm) in from either side, and ¹⁄₁₆" (2 mm) from the top of the sheet. Punch a hole through each mark using the hole-punch pliers. Use one end of the copper wire to form a wrapped loop through one of the holes; repeat using the other end of the wire and the other punched hole, creating a large crescent shape.

FIGURE 1

MATERIALS

I call these pieces "found objects" because there are those little antique pieces we're drawn to and must have with no idea of how we'll use them. Go through your junk drawer and see what you can find to punch into.

2½" (6.5 cm) brass bangle

12-gauge 10mm OD brass jump rings (as many as you need to attach your found objects)

TOOLS

Brass mallet

Bench block

Fine-point permanent marker

#0000 steel wool

Screw-down hole punch

Chain-nose pliers

Flat-nose pliers

PUNCHES

Whistle charm:

"V"

Brass Bezel:

Small Curve—Parenthesis, Short Dash, Slash

Bangle:

4 Petal—Cross Star, Period

TECHNIQUES

Punching

Patinating

Hole punching

SULLIVAN FOUND OBJECTS

I am always seeking out the local bead shops and bead shows when I travel; I find these environments to be among my favorite places. While treasure hunting I am always drawn to raw brass trinkets. I have collected tons of these little gems over the years, and I finally figured out what to do with them. Adding a little freehand-punched pattern onto the smooth surface of these treasures make them come alive. The only rule when making this style of punched jewelry is to be careful you're not punching steel objects. This will cause your steel design stamps to become dull.

BEGINNER　　　　　**PUNCH PATTERN FREEHAND**

PUNCH THE FOUND OBJECTS

1 Examine your pieces and decide where you want to punch your design. Look at your design stamps and see which designs will fit into the spaces. I start on the center of an area and then build from there. You may find this helpful when laying out your plan. Freehand stamp designs onto each found object and the bangle bracelet.

DARKEN THE IMPRESSIONS

2 Darken the punched impressions with a permanent marker. Remove any excess marker off the top surface of the metal with steel wool.

PUNCH THE HOLES

3 For the trinkets used in this bracelet, I used the large side of the screw-down hole punch to punch my holes so that they would accommodate 12-gauge jump rings.

ATTACH THE FOUND OBJECTS TO THE BANGLE

4 Use jump rings to attach the found objects to the bangle bracelet.

ADDITIONAL TECHNIQUES

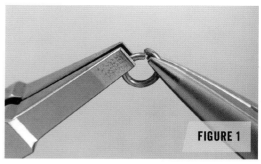

FIGURE 1

OPENING AND CLOSING JUMP RINGS

When opening and closing jump rings, use chain- and flat-nose pliers. Grip both sides of the jump ring on either side of the seam with the pliers (**Figure 1**) and twist or swivel the jump ring open or closed (**Figure 2**). When closing jump rings, you sometimes need to overcompensate for a springiness in the metal by twisting the ends past each other just a little bit (**Figure 3**); they will settle into alignment once you release the pressure from the pliers. Do not pry the jump ring open into a "C" shape.

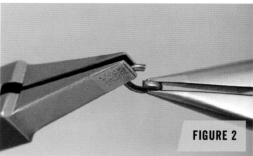

FIGURE 2

FORMING A SIMPLE LOOP

To form a simple loop, use flat-nose pliers to make a 90-degree bend at least ½" (1.3 cm) from the end of the wire. Use round-nose pliers to grasp the wire after the bend; roll the pliers toward the bend, but not past it, to preserve the 90-degree bend. Use your thumb to continue the wrap around the nose of the pliers. Trim the wire next to the bend. Open a simple loop just as you would a jump ring.

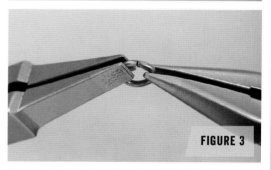

FIGURE 3

FORMING A WRAPPED LOOP

To form a wrapped loop, begin with a 90-degree bend at least 2" (5 cm) away from the end of the wire. Use round-nose pliers to form a simple loop with a tail overlapping the bend. Wrap the tail tightly.

SIMPLE LOOP

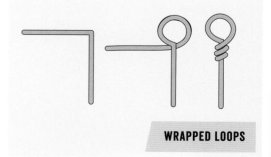

WRAPPED LOOPS

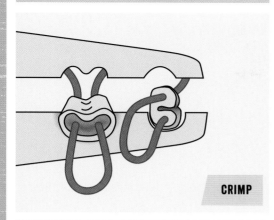

CRIMP

CRIMPING

Crimp tubes are seamless metal tubes used to secure the end of a beading wire. To use, string a crimp tube and the connection finding (i.e., the loop of the clasp). Pass back through the tube, leaving a short tail. Use the back notch of the crimping pliers to press the length of the tube down between the wires, enclosing them in separate chambers of the crescent shape. Rotate the tube 90 degrees and use the front notch of the pliers to fold the two chambers onto themselves, forming a clean cylinder. Crimping pliers are shown here, but you may prefer using chain-nose pliers to simply flatten your crimps. Trim the excess wire.

Crimp covers hide crimp tubes and give your piece a professional finish. To attach, gently hold a crimp cover in the front notch of the crimping pliers. Insert the crimped tube and gently squeeze the pliers, encasing the tube inside the cover.

OVERHAND KNOT

This is the basic knot for tying off thread. Make a loop with the stringing material. Pass the cord that lies behind the loop over the front cord and through the loop; pull snug.

FINDING YOUR RING-BAND SIZE

Follow these steps to calculate exactly how much sheet metal you need to make a ring band that fits you. Find the inner circumference of your ring size on the chart on page 86 (Vermillion Ring). Multiply the thickness of your metal sheet in millimeters by three and add that figure to the inner circumference measurement to get the length of metal you need to cut. The width of your ring band is a matter of personal preference and can be as wide or narrow as you would like to make it.

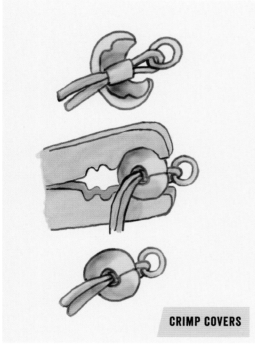

CRIMP COVERS

OVERHAND KNOT

CONVERSION CHART

B & S Gauge	MM	Inches Decimals
10	2.59	1.02
12	2.05	.081
14	1.63	.064
16	1.29	.051
18	1.02	.040
20	.812	.032
22	.644	.025
24	.511	.020

PUNCH PATTERNS

PHOTOCOPY ALL PUNCH PATTERNS AT 100%.

PUNCH PATTERN 1

PUNCH PATTERN 2

PUNCH PATTERN 3

PUNCH PATTERN 4

PUNCH PATTERN 5

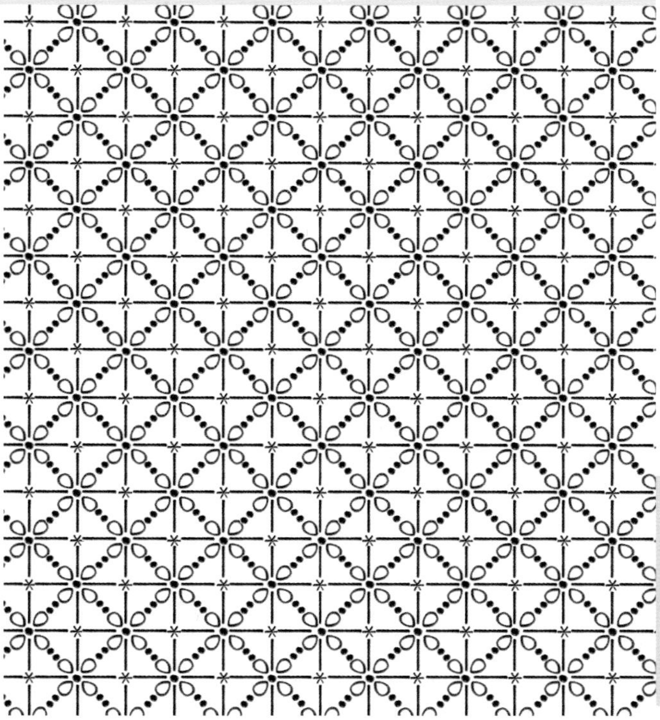

PUNCH PATTERN 6

PUNCH PATTERN 7

PUNCH PATTERN 8

TEMPLATES

PHOTOCOPY TEMPLATES AT 100%.

HALF-MOON BEAD CAPS

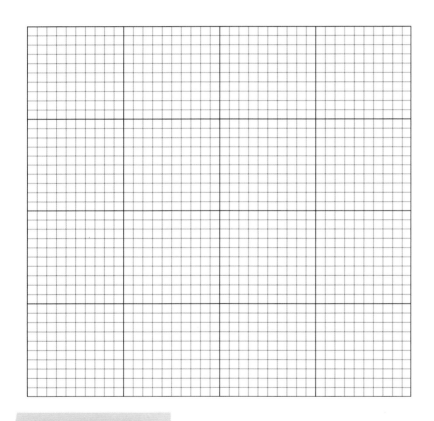

GRAPH PAPER PATTERN

TAMARAC HOOP EARRINGS

SYLVIA SHRINE NECKLACE

BELLE PENDANT

CALHOUN TILES BRACELET

JOSEPHINE CRESCENT NECKLACE

HARRIET BOUQUET NECKLACE

RESOURCES

BEADUCATION

beaducation.com
(650) 261-1870
Tools and materials: metal blanks, plastic templates, steel design stamps, sheet metal, tools, and wire

BEADWORK SUPPLIES

beadwork-supplies.com
(712) 256-3207
5" × 1" (12.5 × 2.5 cm) scalloped necklace blank used in the Harriet Bouquet Necklace project

BROOKLYN CHARM

brooklyncharmshop.com
145 Bedford Ave.
Brooklyn, NY 11211
(347) 689-2492
Brass charms

DAKOTA STONES

dakotastones.com
(612) 298-7371
Stone beads

FUSION BEADS

fusionbeads.com
(888) 781-3559
Beading wire, crimps, findings, and seed beads

LAVEO BEADS

etsy.com/shop/laveobeads
Stone pendants

METALLIFEROUS

metalliferous.com
(212) 944-0909
Sheet metal and bangle blanks

NUNN DESIGN

nunndesign.com
(360) 379-3557
Finished Patera bezels

SUBLIME STITCHING

sublimestitching.com
Embroidery patterns

WARG ENAMEL AND TOOL CENTER

wargetc.com
(207) 885-9382
Circle divider

2 MOON TOOLS

etsy.com/shop/2moontools
2moontools@gmail.com
Steel design stamps

INDEX

DESIGN SOPHISTICATED
METAL JEWELRY
WITH THESE CREATIVE RESOURCES FROM INTERWEAVE

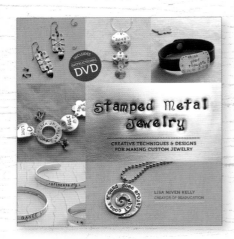

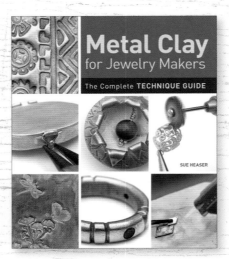

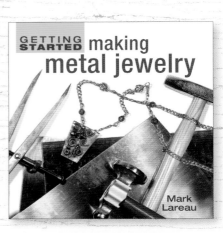

STAMPED METAL JEWELRY
Creative Techniques & Designs for
Making Custom Jewelry
Lisa Niven Kelly
ISBN 978-1-59668-177-4
$24.95

METAL CLAY FOR JEWELRY MAKERS
The Complete Technique Guide
Sue Heaser
ISBN 978-1-59668-713-4
$29.95

**GETTING STARTED
MAKING METAL JEWELRY**
Mark Lareau
ISBN 978-1-59668-025-8
$19.95

AVAILABLE AT YOUR FAVORITE RETAILER OR

 Jewelry Making Daily *Shop*
shop.jewelrymakingdaily.com

LAPIDARY JOURNAL
JEWELRY
ARTIST

Check out *Jewelry Artist,* a trusted guide to the
art of gems, jewelry making, design, beads,
minerals, and more. Whether you are a beginner,
an experienced artisan, or in the jewelry business,
Jewelry Artist can take you to a whole new level.
Jewelryartistmagazine.com

 Jewelry Making Daily

Jewelry Making Daily is the ultimate online
community for anyone interested in creating
handmade jewelry. Get tips from industry experts,
download free step-by-step projects, check out
video demos, discover sources for supplies, and
more! Sign up at **jewelrymakingdaily.com**.